CW01637230

AGE
13-14
Key Stage 3

national TESTS
practice papers
FOR THE YEAR 2002

Maths, English and Science

Book 2

practice Papers

Contents

Page

Acknowledgements
The authors and publisher would like to thank the following for permission to reproduce material in this book.

Portrait of the Artist as a Young Dog, Dylan Thomas, J.M. Dent and Sons Ltd and the Trustees for the copyright of the late Dylan Thomas.

'Warning' by Jenny Joseph, from *A Rose in the Afternoon*, J.M. Dent and Sons Ltd.

Every effort has been made to trace and acknowledge ownership of copyright material but if any have been inadvertently overlooked, the publisher will be pleased to make the necessary alterations at the first opportunity.

First published 2001
exclusively for WHSmith by

Hodder & Stoughton Educational,
a division of Hodder Headline Ltd
338 Euston Road
London NW1 3BH

Text and illustrations © Hodder & Stoughton Educational 2001

All rights reserved. No part of this publication may be reproduced or transmitted in any form or by any means, electronic or mechanical, including photocopying, recording or any information storage and retrieval system, without permission in writing from the publisher.

A CIP record for this book is available from the British Library.

Authors: Steve Mills and Hilary Koll (Maths), Christine Moorcroft and Ray Barker (English), Terry Hudson (Science)

ISBN 0340 84587 2

Printed and bound by Graphycems, Spain

NOTE: The tests, questions and advice in this book are not reproductions of the official test materials sent to schools. The official testing process is supported by guidance and training for teachers in setting and marking tests and interpreting the results. The results achieved in the tests in this book may not be the same as are achieved in the official tests.

The National Tests: A Summary

What are the National Tests?

Children who attend state schools in England and Wales sit National Tests (commonly known as SATs) at the ages of 7, 11 and 14, usually at the beginning of May. They may also sit optional tests in the intervening years – many schools have chosen to adopt these tests. The test results are accompanied by an assessment by the child's teacher (at Key Stage 3 this also covers non-tested subjects such as History or Geography).

The results are used by the school to assess each child's level of knowledge and progress in English and Maths at Key Stage 1 and English, Maths and Science at Key Stages 2 and 3. They also provide useful guidance for the child's next teacher when he or she is planning the year's work.

The educational calendar for children aged 5–14 is structured as follows:

Key Stage	Year	Age by end of year	National Test
1 (KS1)	1	6	
	2	7	KEY STAGE 1
	3	8	Optional Year 3
2 (KS2)	4	9	Optional Year 4
	5	10	Optional Year 5
	6	11	KEY STAGE 2
3 (KS3)	7	12	
	8	13	
	9	14	KEY STAGE 3

Timetable

Key Stage 3 students will sit their tests on **7–13 May 2002**, with the following timetable (check with the school as dates may change):

Tuesday 7 May	**Wednesday 8 May**	**Thursday 9 May**	**Friday 10 May**	**Monday 13 May**
		MORNING		
English Paper 1 ($1\frac{1}{2}$ hours plus 15 minutes reading time)	Mathematics Paper 1 (1 hour)	English Extension Paper ($1\frac{1}{2}$ hours)	Science Paper 1 (1 hour)	Science Extension Paper (1 hour)
	Mental Arithmetic Tests A and C (20 minutes)	Mental Arithmetic Test B (20 minutes)		
		AFTERNOON		
English Paper 2 ($1\frac{1}{4}$ hours)	Mathematics Paper 2 (1 hour)	Mathematics Extension Paper (1 hour)	Science Paper 2 (1 hour)	

Levels

National targets have been set for students' results in the National Tests, as follows:

LEVEL	AGE 7 (Key Stage 1)	AGE 11 (Key Stage 2)	AGE 14 (Key Stage 3)
8			
7			
6			
5			
4			
3			
2 2a 2b 2c			
1			

BELOW EXPECTED LEVEL

EXPECTED LEVEL

ABOVE EXPECTED LEVEL

EXCEPTIONAL

Results

Your child's school will send you a report indicating his or her levels in the tests and the teacher assessment.

The school's overall test results will be included in local and national league tables, which are published in most newspapers.

What can parents do to help?

While it is never a good idea to encourage cramming, you can help your child to succeed by:

- Making sure he or she has enough food, sleep and leisure time during the test period.
- Practising important skills such as writing and reading, spelling and mental arithmetic.
- Telling him or her what to expect in the test, such as important symbols and key words.
- Helping him or her to be comfortable in test conditions including working within a time limit, reading questions carefully and understanding different ways of answering.

Maths at Key Stage 3

Guidance for parents

The Key Stage 3 National Test in Maths consists of two written papers, one to be taken without a calculator and the other with a calculator, and a mental arithmetic test. The tests will cover aspects of Number and Algebra, Shape, Space and Measures and Handling Data.

Levels and tiers of entry

Your child will be entered for one of four tiers. Your child's teacher will make a judgement about which of the tiers to enter your child for.

This book includes two written papers that cover the most popular tiers of entry. Paper 1 covers levels 4–6 and Paper 2 covers levels 5–7. The mental arithmetic test includes questions at levels 4–7. To gain an idea of the level at which your child is working, use the table on page 47.

Setting the Maths Tests

Equipment needed

Paper 1: pen, pencil, ruler, rubber,

Paper 2: pen, pencil, ruler, rubber, protractor or angle measurer, pair of compasses, scientific or graphic calculator, tracing paper and a mirror (optional).

Mental Maths Test: pencil and rubber.

A clock or watch with a second hand is useful for ensuring times for each question on the mental test are appropriate.

The written papers

A formula sheet is included for each test. Encourage your child to refer to it where necessary. Each written paper lasts for **1 hour**, starting with easier questions and gradually becoming more difficult.

The mental maths test

The mental test should take approximately **20 minutes** to give. Cut out pages 35 to 36 so you can read them aloud to your child. Your child should use the sheets on pages 34, 37 and 38 for his or her answers.

Marking the tests

Next to each question in the written tests is a number indicating how many marks the question or part of the question is worth. Enter your child's mark into the circle above, using the answer pages (39–46) to help you decide how many points to award.

The answer pages also offer advice, provide information about common errors made by pupils and include tips to help your child understand the mathematical ideas.

Find your child's total score from the written papers and refer to page 47 for information about the level at which your child might be working.

Maths Test
Paper 1

You *cannot* use a calculator for any questions in Paper 1.

Formulae

You might need to use these formulae.

AREA

Circle

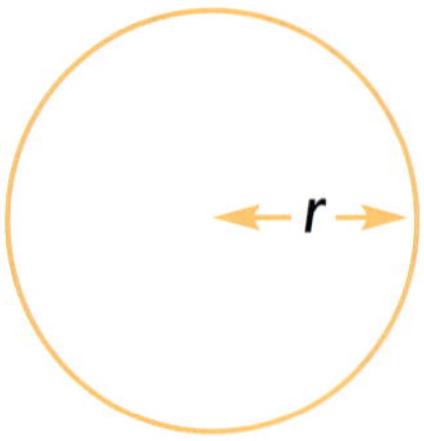

πr^2

Take π as 3.14.

Triangle

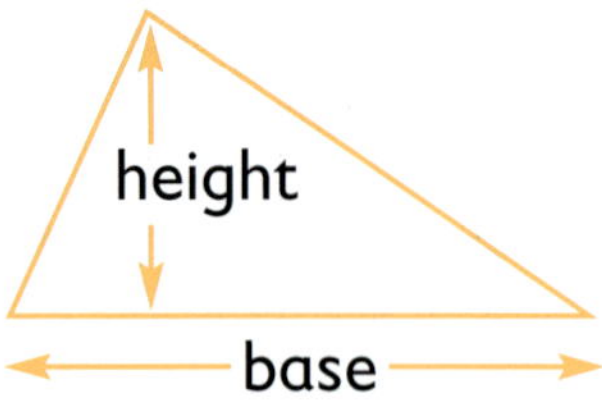

$\dfrac{\text{base} \times \text{height}}{2}$

Parallelogram

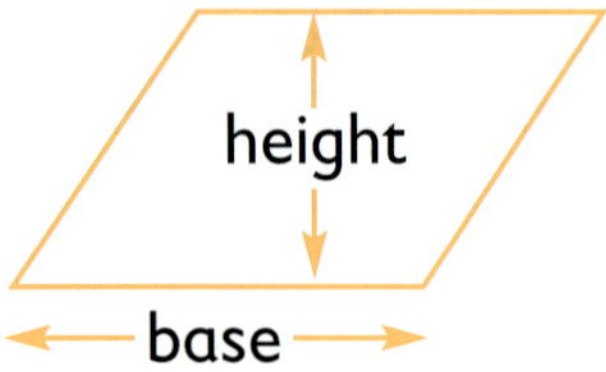

base $\times$ height

Trapezium

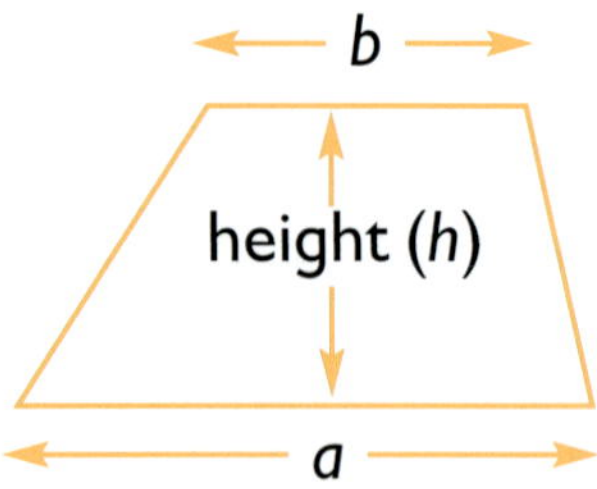

$\dfrac{(a + b)}{2} \times h$

LENGTH

Circle

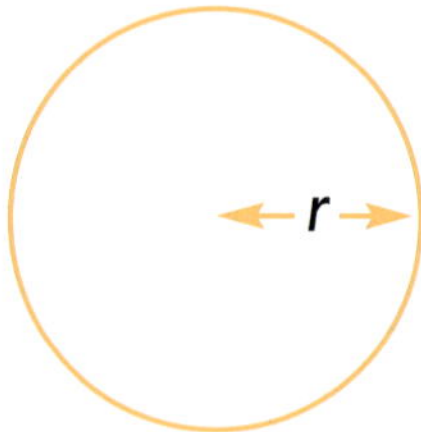

circumference = $2 \pi r$

VOLUME

Prism

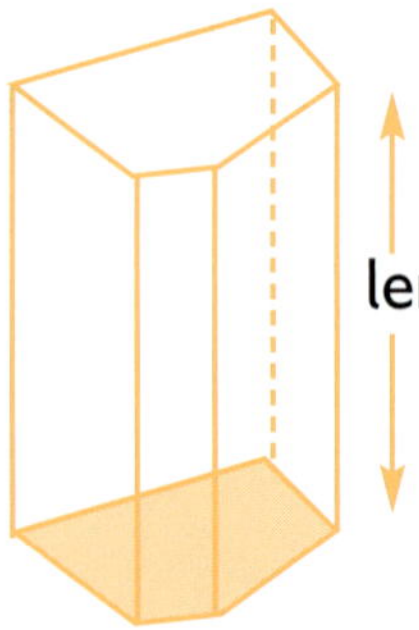

area of cross-section $\times$ length

You will need: pen, pencil, rubber, ruler.

Write one number in each box to make each equation correct.

Example

144 + 30 = **174**

a 168 + 40 = ☐

b 835 − 40 = ☐

c 100 − ☐ = 72

d 10 × ☐ = 420

Maths Test

Paper 1

Calculations

1 Write one number in each box to make each equation correct.

a $34 \times \square = 3400$ 1

b $900 \div \square = 150$ 1

c $\square - 50 = 78$ 1

d $\square \times 6 = 360$ 1

e $\square \div 4 = 12$ 1

TOTAL 5

Shape symmetry

2 A square has **4 lines of reflective symmetry:**

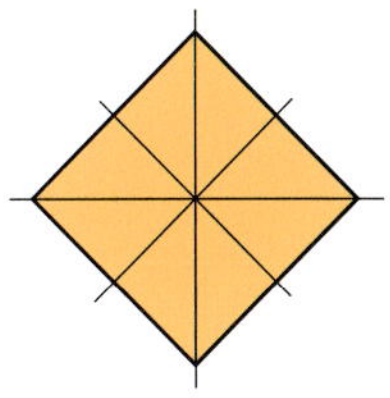

and has **rotational symmetry of order 4:**

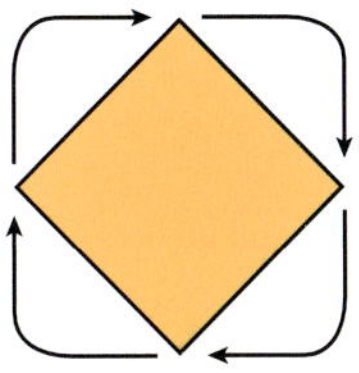

Here are some shapes.

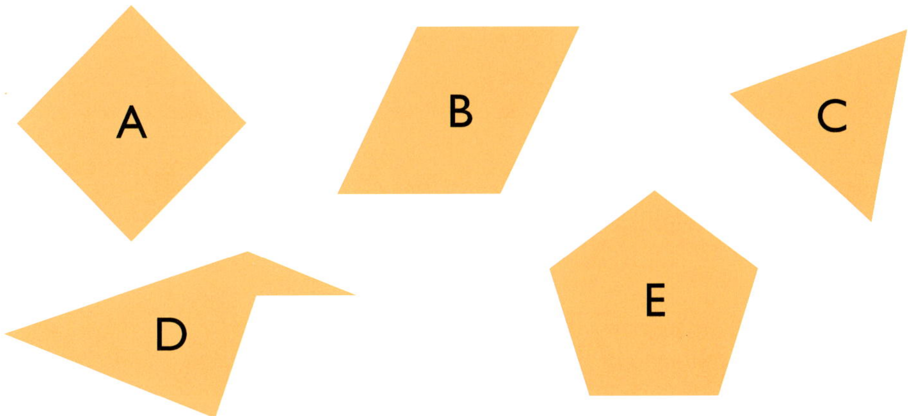

Fill in the missing numbers in the table below.

	lines of reflective symmetry	rotational symmetry of order
Shape A	**4**	**4**
Shape B		
Shape C		
Shape D		
Shape E		

4

TOTAL

4

Canes

3 In a shop, some lengths of cane are being measured with a metre stick. Here are three canes labelled A, B and C.

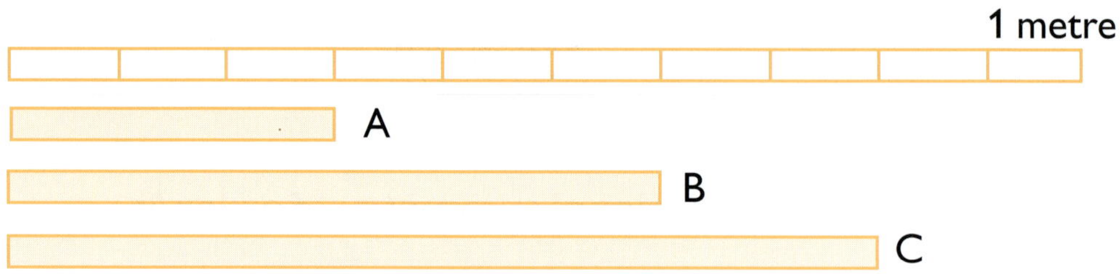

a What fraction of a metre is Cane A?

1

b What fraction of a metre is Cane B?
Give your answer in its simplest form.

1

c What percentage of a metre is Cane C?

1

TOTAL

3

d Another cane, Cane D, is exactly $\frac{2}{5}$ of a metre.

Give the length of Cane D in centimetres.

Cane D = ____________________ cm

1

e Mr Kumar buys 10 pieces of **Cane A**.
If these canes were placed end-to-end in a straight line, how long would the line be?

1

f Another cane, Cane E, is $\frac{2}{3}$ of a metre.

One of the statements below is true. Tick the true statement.

Cane E is shorter than Cane B.	
Cane E is longer than Cane C.	
Cane E is longer than Cane B but shorter than Cane C.	
Cane E is shorter than Cane B but longer than Cane A.	

1

TOTAL

3

School trip

4a A teacher collects money from pupils for a school residential trip.
Each pupil pays **12** instalments of **£10.25**.
What is the total amount of money each pupil pays for the trip?

£

1

b Each pupil takes exactly **£20** spending money on the school trip.
There are **30** pupils.
How much spending money do the pupils take in total?

£

1

c **19** pupils buy an ice cream.
The ice creams cost **50p**.
How much money do they spend on ice creams in total?

£

1

TOTAL

3

d Leroy spends **£8.48** on a T-shirt.
He pays with a **£20** note.
How much change does he get?

1

e Claire writes down how much she spent while on the trip.

Ice creams	**£1.50**
T-shirt	**£8.48**
Cap	**£4.99**
Sweets	**83p**

How much did she spend in total?

£

1

TOTAL

2

Bags of money

5 A bag of money contains different coins.

It has **six 20p** coins, **three 10p** coins, **two 5p** coins and a **1p coin**.

a What is the **probability** that one coin picked from the bag at random is a **1p**? Write your answer as a **fraction**.

1

b Draw a cross on this line to show the probability that the coin is a 20p.

1

impossible **certain**

c Draw a cross on this line to show the probability that the coin is <u>not</u> a 5p.

1

impossible **certain**

TOTAL

3

d Draw a cross on this line to show the probability that the coin is a silver coin.

impossible **certain**

1

Davina decides to pick a coin, record it and **put the coin back**. She does this **60 times**. She organises her results into a table.

Coin	Frequency
20p	29
10p	12
5p	13
1p	6

e Davina looks at her results and says:

"There is a greater probability of picking a 5p coin than a 10p."

Explain why Davina is **wrong**.

1

TOTAL

2

Fishy problems

6 Sam has some tropical fish in a large tank.

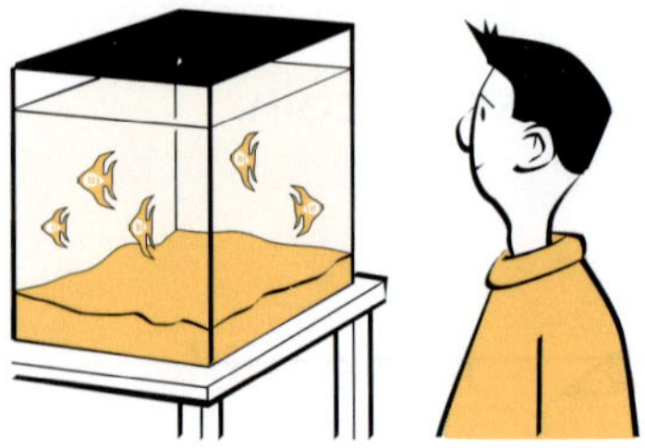

Call the number of fish he has ***n***.

a Sam puts 4 more fish into the tank.

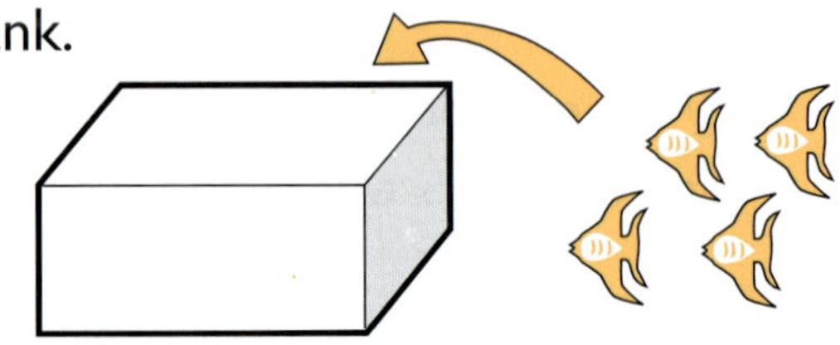

Write an expression to show how many fish are now in the tank.

____

1

b Sam takes the new fish out so that he starts again with ***n*** fish in his tank.

He takes out exactly **one half** of the fish in the tank and puts them into a bowl.

Write an expression to show how many fish are now in the tank.

____

1

TOTAL

2

Sam starts again with ***n*** fish in the tank.

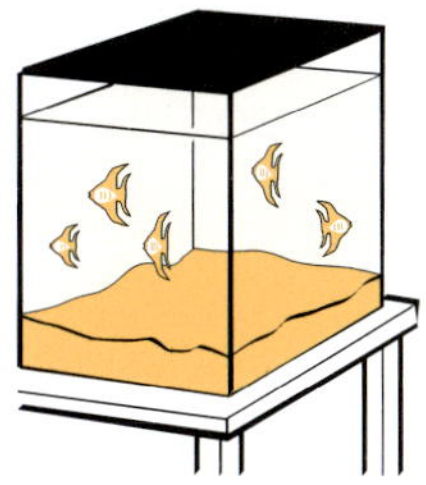

c Write an expression to show how many fish Sam would have if he had **double** this number of fish.

______________________ 1

d Sam's dad has exactly **20 times** as many fish as Sam has.
Write an expression to show how many fish Sam's dad has.

______________________ 1

e These expressions show how many fish are in these two tanks.

Tank A

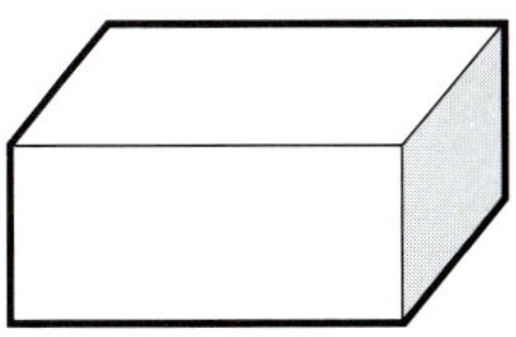

$3n - 3$

Tank B

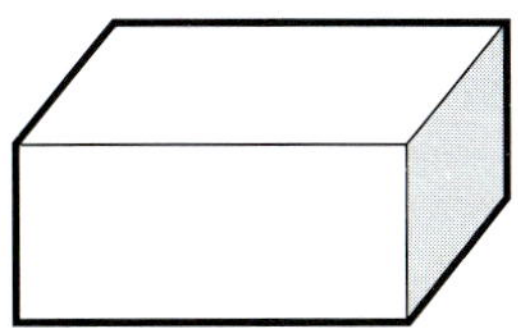

$3(n - 3)$

Do the tanks hold the same amount?
Explain your answer.

____

____

______________________ 1

TOTAL 3

Sequences

7 Here is a sequence of shapes made from white and coloured triangles.

Shape 1 Shape 2 Shape 3 Shape 4

a Complete the table by filling in the missing numbers for Shape **7** and Shape **10.**

Shape number	1	2	3	4	**7**	**10**
Number of coloured triangles	3	5	7	9		
Number of white triangles	1	4	9	16		

2

b Complete the table by writing **expressions** for Shape ***n***.

Shape number	1	2	3	4	**n**
Number of coloured triangles	3	5	7	9	
Number of white triangles	1	4	9	16	

2

TOTAL

4

c Write an expression to show the **total** number of triangles used to make Shape ***n***. **Simplify** your expression.

1

d For a different sequence of shapes, the number of **squares** used can be expressed as $2n + 3$.

Which of the sets of shapes below shows Shapes 1 and 2 in this sequence?

Set 1

Shape 1 Shape 2

Set 2

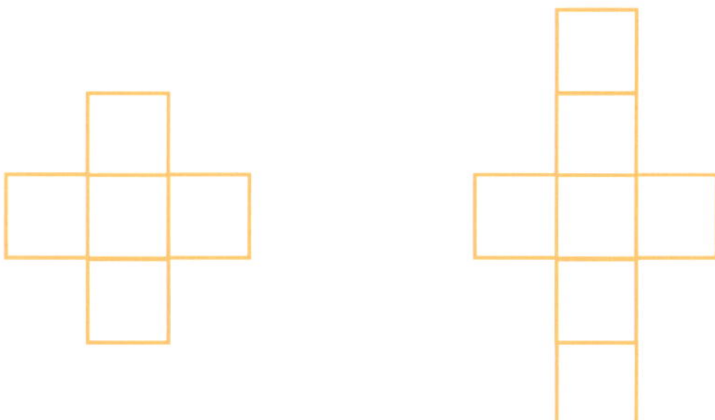

Shape 1 Shape 2

Set 3

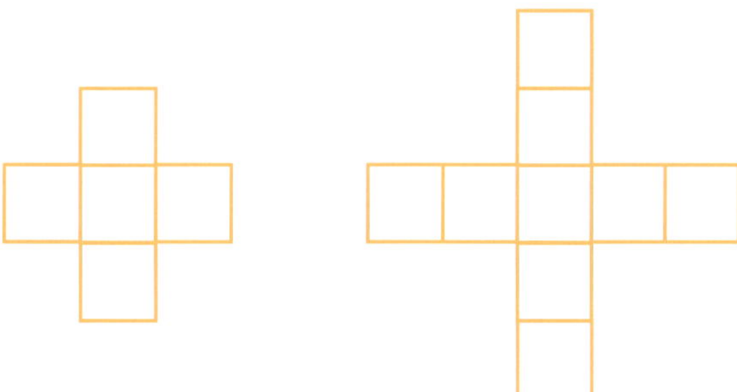

Shape 1 Shape 2

Set ____________________

1

TOTAL

2

Angles

8 This shape is part of a design.

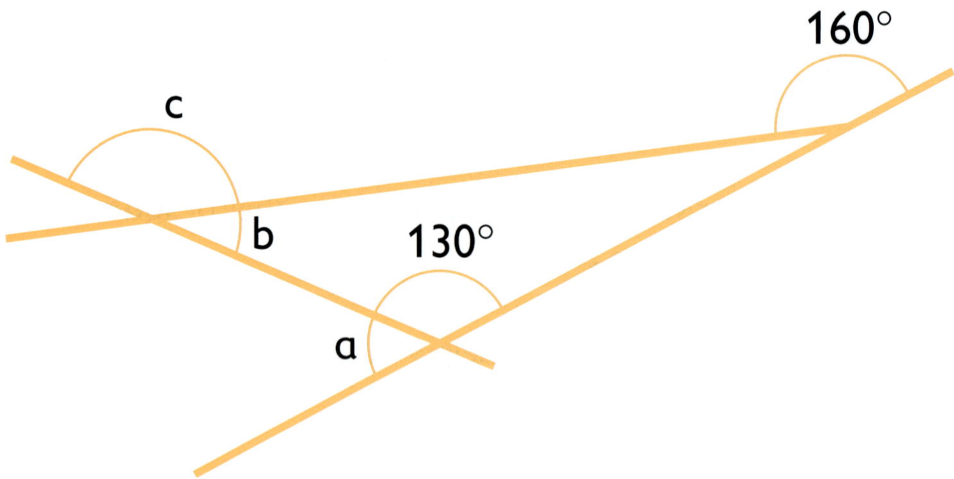

Calculate angles a, b and c.

$a =$ ______ °

$b =$ ______ °

$c =$ ______ °

3

TOTAL

3

Linear equations

9 Aswin has been plotting some lines on a graph.
The line AB is **parallel** to the line CD.

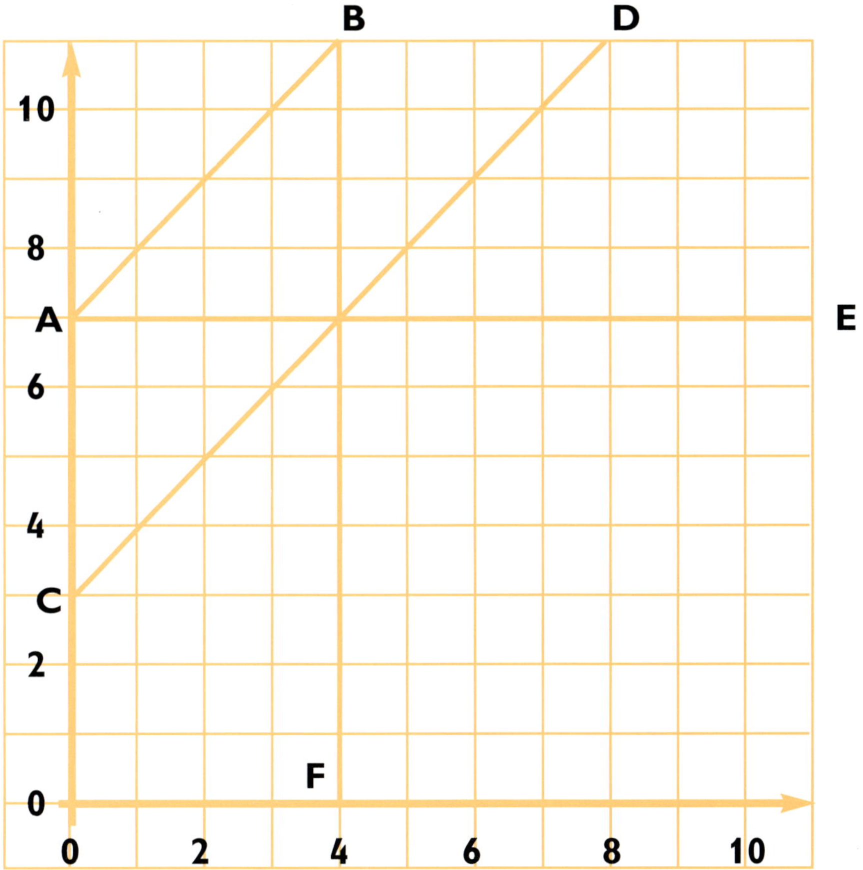

a The equation of the line BF is $x = 4$.
What is the equation of the line AE?

1

b The line AB has the equation $y = x + 7$.
What is the equation of the line CD?

1

c On the graph, draw and label the line GH with the equation
$y = -x + 10$

1

TOTAL

3

Areas

10 Here are two shapes. They are not drawn to scale.
The area of the trapezium is **three times** the area of the parallelogram.

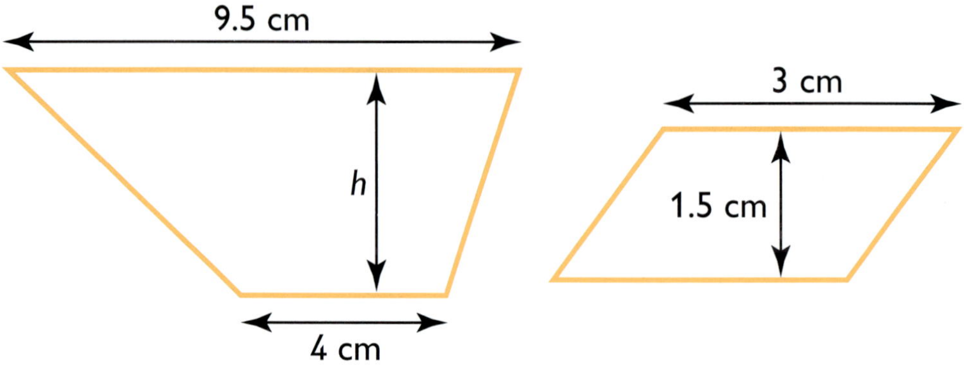

a Calculate the height of the trapezium (h).
Show your working.

2

h = ... cm

b What is the area of the trapezium below?
Give your answer in terms of y, in its simplest form.

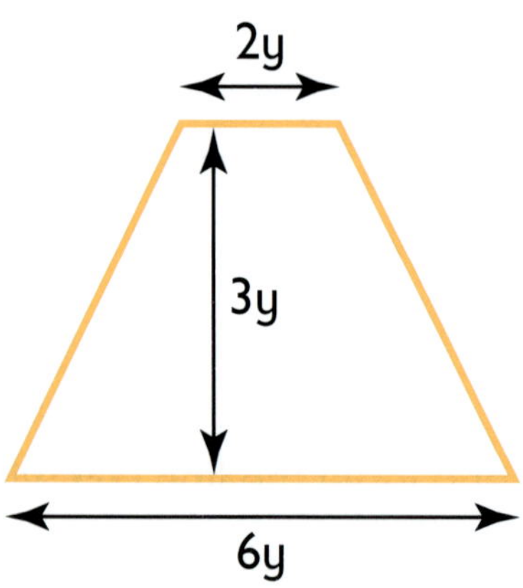

Area = ____________________

1

TOTAL

3

Formulae

You *can* use a calculator for any questions in Paper 2.

You might need to use these formulae.

AREA

Circle

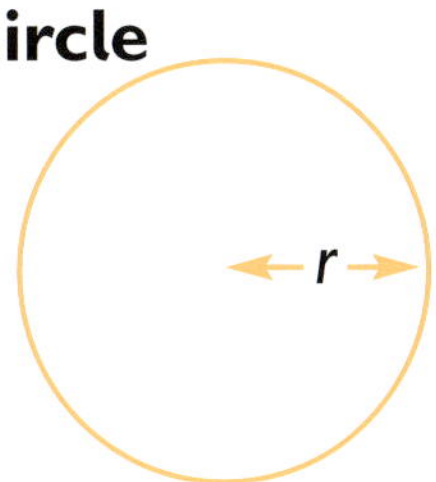

πr^2

Take π as 3.14 or use the π button on your calculator.

Triangle

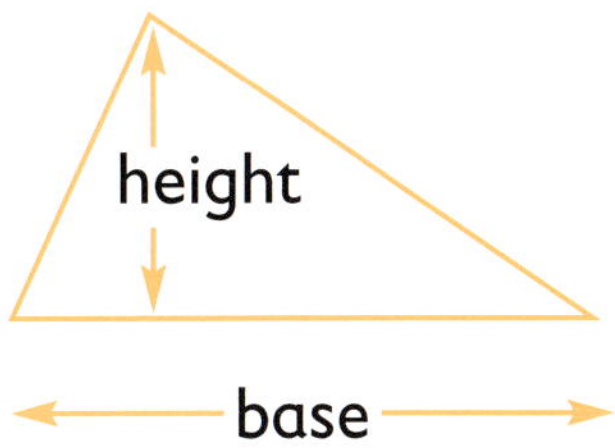

$\dfrac{\text{base} \times \text{height}}{2}$

Parallelogram

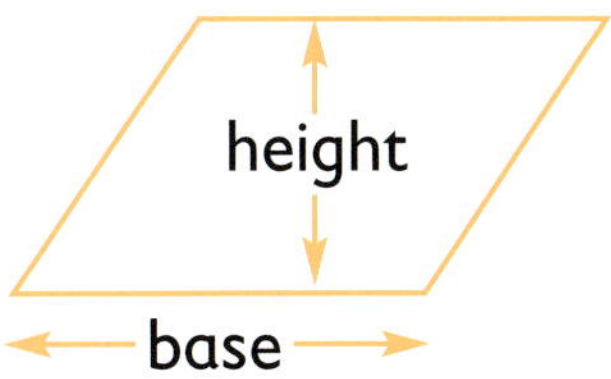

base × height

Trapezium

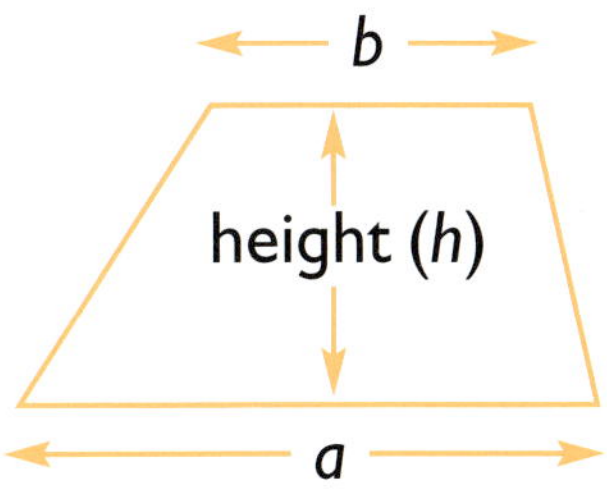

$\dfrac{(a + b)}{2} \times h$

LENGTH

Circle

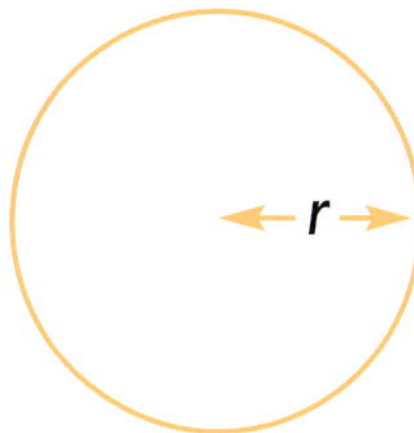

circumference = $2\pi r$

For a right-angled triangle

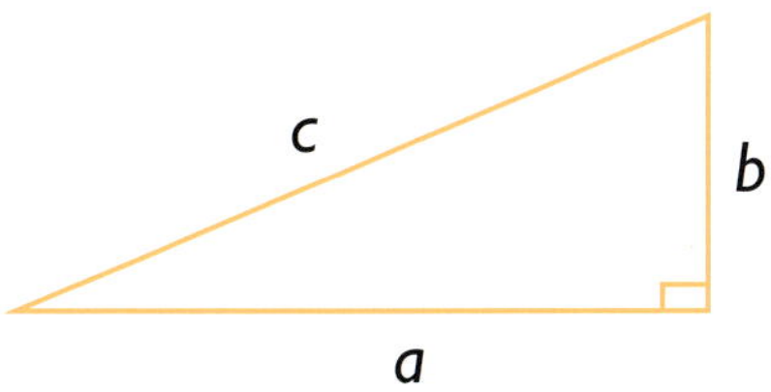

$a^2 + b^2 = c^2$ (Pythagoras' Theorem)

VOLUME

Prism

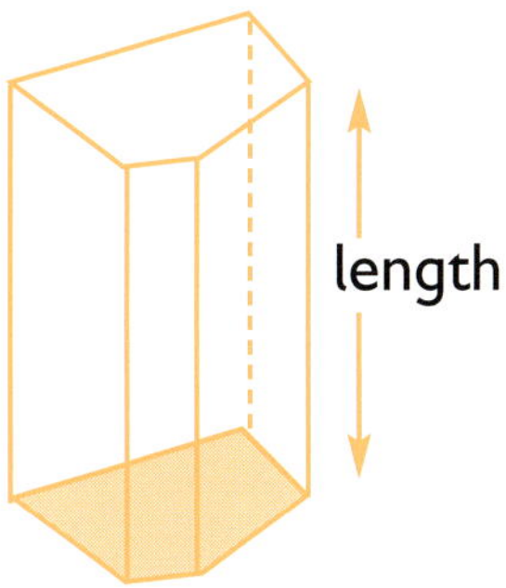

area of cross-section × length

You will need: pen, pencil, rubber, ruler, scientific or graphic calculator, a pair of compasses, proctractor, tracing paper, mirror (optional).

Running

1 This graph shows the progress of two runners during a 60 metre race.

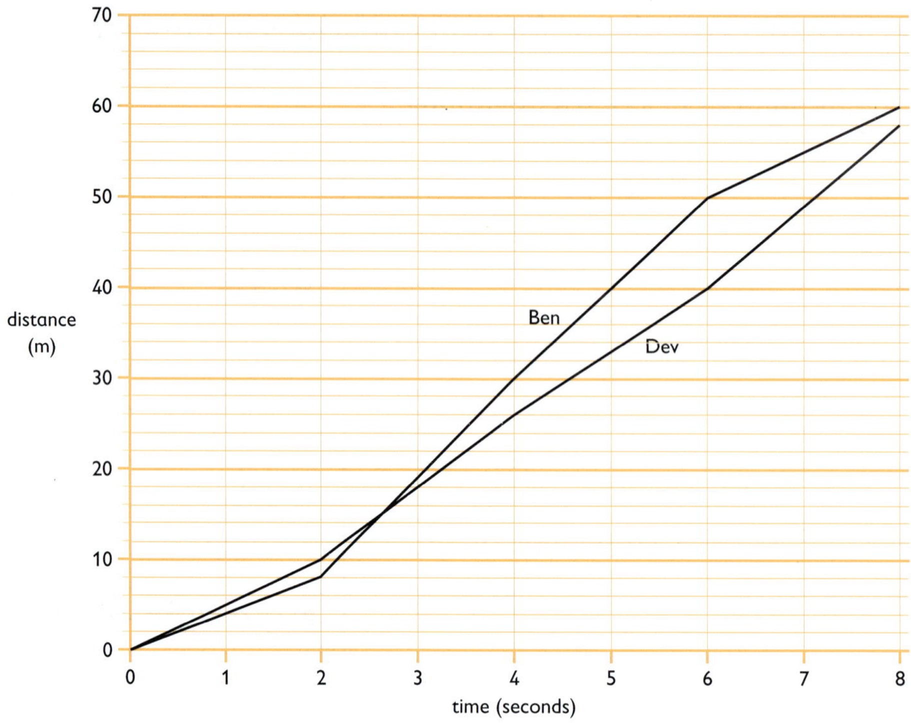

a This table shows the progress of **Dev** during the race.
Complete the table, using the graph above.

Seconds	distance at start (m)	distance at end (m)	running rate (m)
0–2	0	10	10
2–4	10	26	16
4–6			
6–8			

2

TOTAL

2

This table shows the progress of **Ben** during the race.

Seconds	distance at start (m)	distance at end (m)	running rate (m)
0–2	0	8	8
2–4	8	30	22
4–6	30	50	20
6–8	50	60	10

b Use the two tables to help you describe the differences in progress between the two runners during the race.

2

c Use the graph to see which of the runners won the 60 m race.

1

TOTAL

3

Square sequences

2 Here is a sequence of shapes made from white and coloured squares.

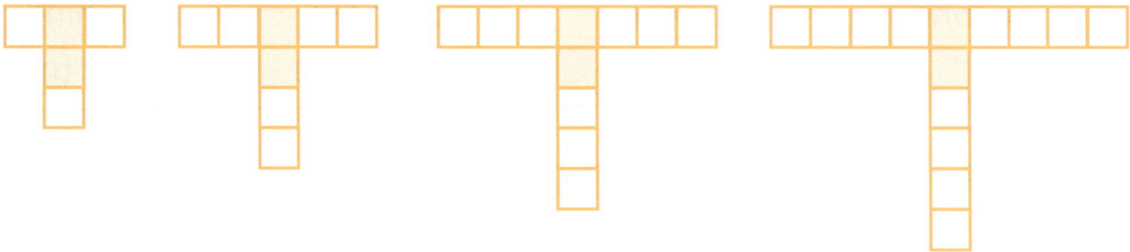

Shape 1 Shape 2 Shape 3 Shape 4

The rule for finding the **number of squares** in **Shape *n*** is

$$3n + 2$$

a Venus says:

"You can see that the pattern is 3n + 2 by studying the shapes."

Explain in your own words what you think Venus means.

____

____

____

1

b How many **white** squares and how many **coloured** squares are in Shape 12?

________ white and ________ coloured squares

2

TOTAL

3

c Shape **3** is made from **11** squares. A shape in this sequence is made from **62** squares. What is the number of this shape?

Shape ______________

1

d Here is a new sequence of shapes made from white and coloured squares.

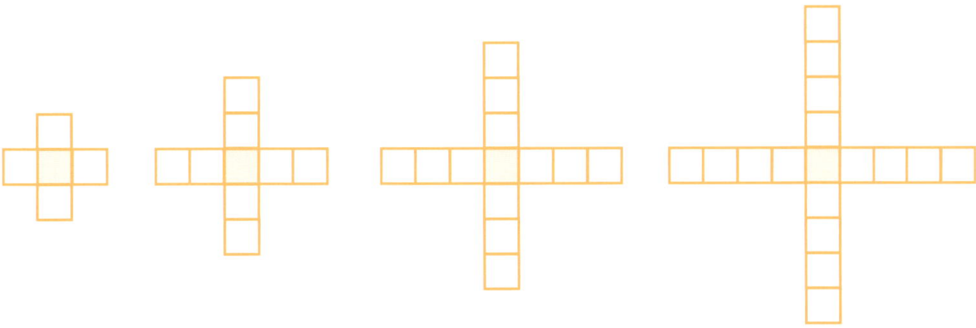

Shape 1 Shape 2 Shape 3 Shape 4

Write a rule for finding the number of squares in **Shape *n***.

Number of squares =

1

TOTAL

2

Cubes

3 Here are two shapes made from small cubes. Three of the cubes are coloured.

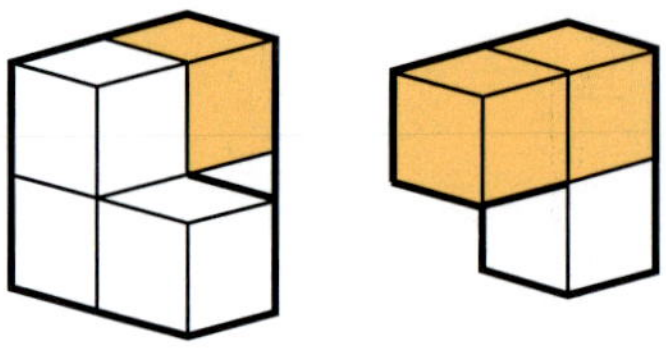

The two shapes are joined together to make a **cuboid**.

a Draw a picture of this **cuboid** on the grid below.
Shade the three coloured cubes on your picture.

2

b Each small cube is one centimetre cubed (1 cm^3).
Write the dimensions of the cuboid you have drawn.

Length = ...cm Width = ...cm Height = ...cm

1

TOTAL

3

Here is a drawing of a different cuboid made from centimetre cubes.

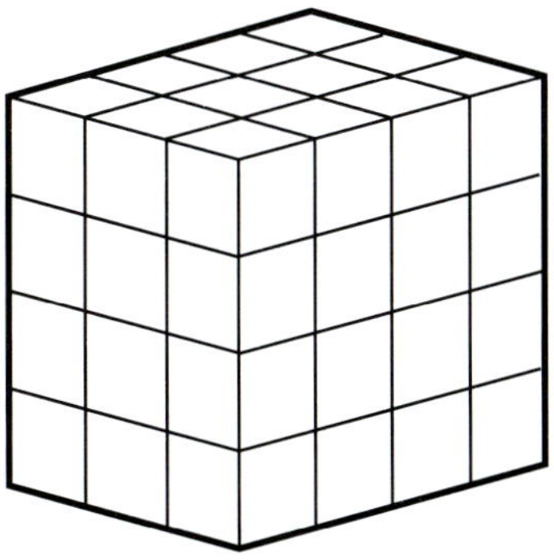

c What is the **volume** of this cuboid?

2

Volume = ... cm^3

d Jo picks up this cuboid. She looks at it from all angles. She realises that some of the small cubes inside the cuboid cannot be seen from any angle.

How many of the small cubes **cannot** be seen?

1

e What fraction of the total number of cubes **can** be seen?

1

TOTAL

4

Volume

4 Jeremy knows that the volume of a cuboid is **268.32 cm^3.**
He knows that the height is 12 cm, and that the length is **6 cm greater** than the width.

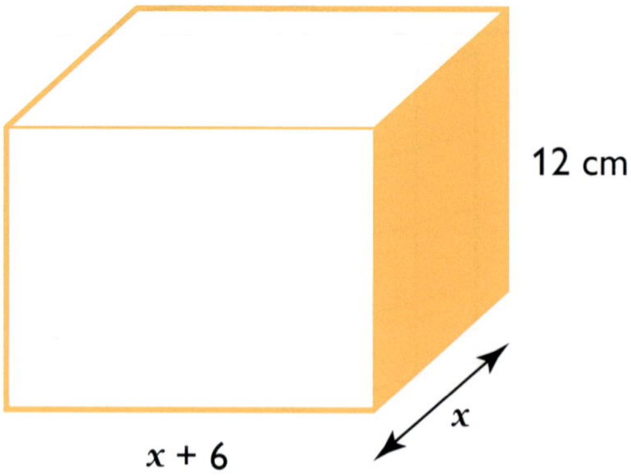

Jeremy writes this equation to show the volume of the cuboid.

$$x(x + 6) \times 12 = 268.32$$

Find the value of x.

You may find this table helpful.

x	$x + 6$	$x(x + 6)$	$x(x + 6) \times 12$	
4	10	40	480	too large

x = ...cm

4

TOTAL

4

Baking

5 When baking cakes, Rob follows this instruction:

2 parts butter to **7 parts flour**

a In one **cake**, Rob uses **350 g** of **flour**.
How much butter does he use?

butter = ______________ g

1

b In a second **cake**, Rob uses **80 g** of **butter**.
How much flour does he use?

flour = ______________ g

1

c Rob makes a third cake. He mixes a total of **1800 g** of **flour and butter**.
How much **flour and butter** does he use?
Show your working.

flour = ______________ g   butter = ______________ g

2

TOTAL

4

Scalene triangle

6 This sketch shows the measurements of a scalene triangle.
Angle *a* is not given.

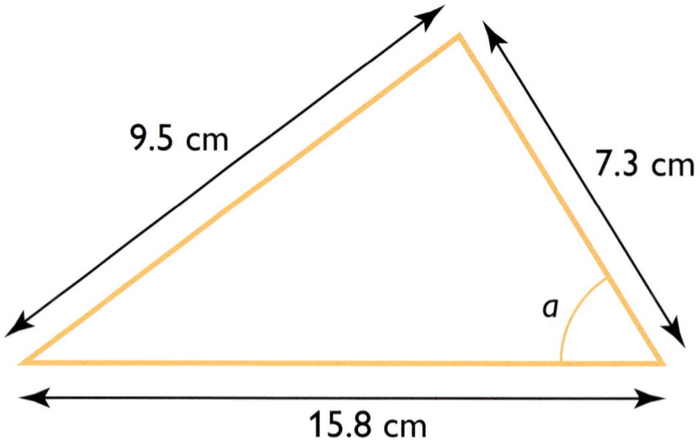

a Make an **accurate** drawing of the triangle.
You may use a ruler and a pair of compasses.

2

b Use a protractor to measure angle *a* to the nearest degree.

a = ... °

1

TOTAL

3

Area and circumference

7a The **diameter** of a circle is **16 cm.**

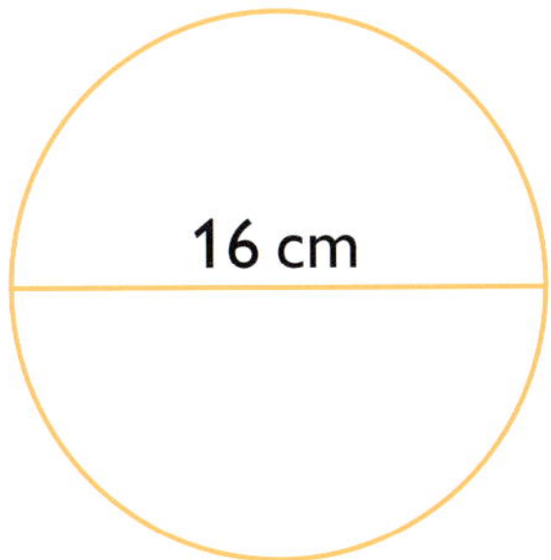

Find the **area** of this circle. Take π to be 3.14.
Show your working.

Area of circle = ...cm^2

2

b The **circumference** of a different circle is **69 cm** to the nearest centimetre.
Find the radius of this circle.
Give your answer to the nearest centimetre.
Show your working.

Radius of circle = ...cm

2

TOTAL

4

Sports Day

8 During Sports Day some students took part in the cricket ball throwing competition. Their results are shown below.

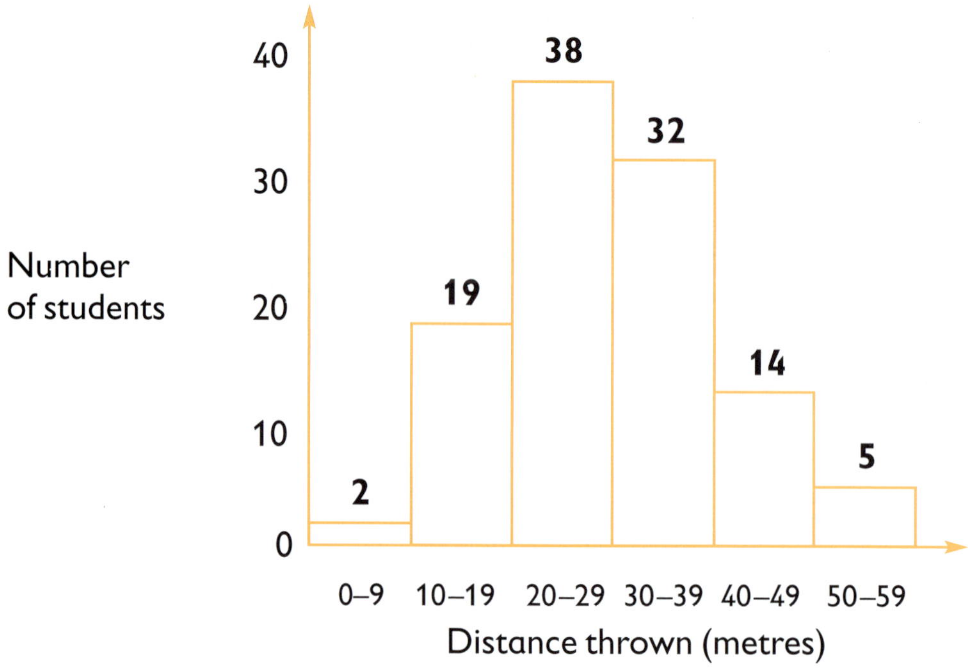

a How many students took part in the competition?

1

b Serena says:
"Less than half of the students threw further than 25 metres."

Do you think Serena's comment is true or false, or do you think more information is needed? Explain your answer.

1

TOTAL

2

c Tanya says:
" The range of the throws is 59."

Do you think Tanya's comment is true or false, or do you think more information is needed? Explain your answer.

____

____

____

1

d Calculate an estimate of the **mean** distance thrown.
Give your answer to 1 decimal place.
You may find this table helpful.

metres	midpoint of bar (x)	number of students (f)	fx
0–9	4.5	2	9
10–19	14.5	19	
20–29	24.5	38	
30–39	34.5	32	
40–49	44.5	14	
50–59	54.5	5	

.... m

2

TOTAL

3

Money matters

9 Lucy and Emily have different amounts of money in whole pounds. Call the number of pounds Lucy has p and the number of pounds Emily has q.

If you multiply Lucy's amount by four and then add two, you get three times Emily's amount.
If you multiply Lucy's amount by eight and then subtract two, you get five times Emily's amount.

Use these statements to write two simultaneous equations and solve them.
Show your working.

p = ... q = ...

4

TOTAL

4

Field

10 Andy and Carol are out walking. They reach a field where a sign says 'Beware of the bull!'. Instead of walking across the field, they decide to walk around the edge.

The field is rectangular with a width of 25 m and a length of 42 m.

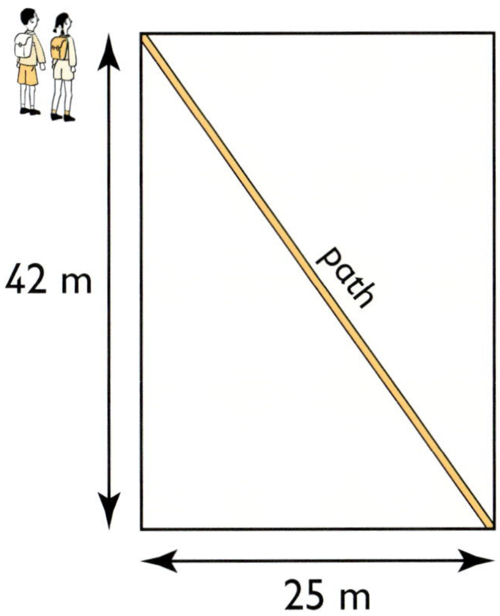

How much further do they walk around the edge than they would walk straight across the field?
Show your working. Give your answer to 2 significant figures.

4

TOTAL

4

Mental Maths test

Answer Sheet

5-second questions

			Marks
1		$\frac{3}{4}$	1
2		23 27	1
3			1
4	millilitres		1
5		$\frac{16}{24}$	1
6		36.27	1

10-second questions

			Marks
7	$p =$	$2p = q$	1
8	%		1
9	cm^2	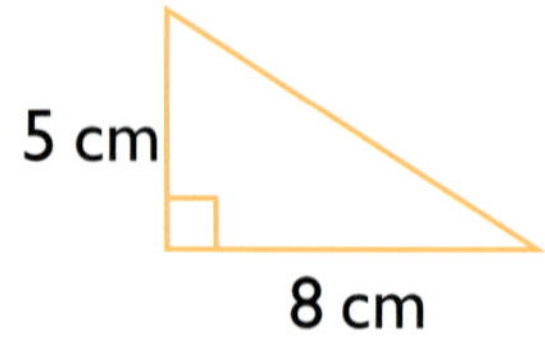	1
10			1

TOTAL

10

"For this first set of questions you have five seconds to work out each answer and write it down."

1 Write three quarters as a decimal.

2 Look at your answer sheet. What is half the total of the numbers shown?

3 What is six thousand multiplied by ten?

4 How many millilitres are there in three litres?

5 Look at your answer sheet. Change the fraction into its simplest form.

6 Write the number thirty six point two seven to one decimal place.

"For the next set of questions you have ten seconds to work out each answer and write it down."

7 Look at the answer sheet. What is the value of *p* when *q* equals five?

8 Fourteen out of twenty goals scored in the Premier League last week were scored in the second half. What percentage of goals were scored in the second half?

9 Look at the answer sheet. What is the area of the triangle?

10 The ratio of adults to children at the swimming pool was two to five. If there were eight adults, how many children were there?

11 Write two numbers that add up to eight point three two.

12 Write a fraction that is equivalent to five sixths.

13 In the high jump, Dan's first jump was one point three metres. His second jump was one point five seven metres. How many centimetres higher was his second jump?

14 Look at the answer sheet. What is the value of eight *y*?

15 The mean of three numbers is ten. Two of the numbers are eight and nine. What is the third number?

16 Look at the answer sheet. Which number is nearest to one and a half?

17 The value of four *a* plus three *b* is twelve. What is the value of eight *a* plus six *b*?

18 Look at the answer sheet. Write a possible value for *s*.

"For the next set of questions you have fifteen seconds to work out each answer and write it down."

19 The difference between *c* and *d* is five. The product of *c* and *d* is thirty six. What are the values of *c* and *d*?

20 Look at the answer sheet. Two hundred people said where they went on holiday last year. About how many people went to France?

21 What is half of three eighths?

22 Write three odd numbers that add up to thirty three.

23 Look at the answer sheet. Use the calculation to help you to answer the question.

24 Look at the answer sheet. The area of the square is *n* squared. What is its perimeter?

25 A megaburger costs one pound forty nine pence. What would five megaburgers cost?

26 Divide four hundred and seventy five by twenty five.

27 Look at the answer sheet. Draw a ring around the largest expression.

28 Look at the answer sheet. The length of this pool is twice the width. The perimeter is eighteen metres. What is the length of the pool?

29 What is four to the power three divided by eight?

30 Look at the answer sheet. Write an expression, in terms of *y*, for z plus two.

11		8.32
12		$\frac{5}{6}$
13	centimetres	
14		$2y = 9$
15		
16		1.4 1.59 1.6 1.42
17		$4a + 3b$ $8a + 6b$
18		$-3 < s < 2$

1
1
1
1
1
1
1
1

15-second questions

19	and	
20		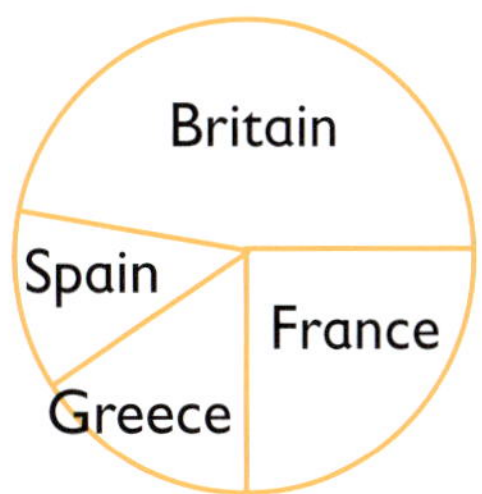

1
1

TOTAL

10

21 | $\frac{3}{8}$

22

23 $32 \times 1.6 =$ | $32 \times 16 = 512$

24

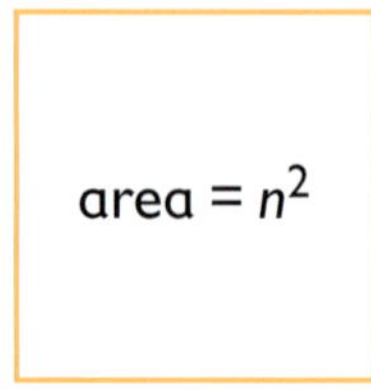

25 £

26

27 | $3^2 + 8$ 4^2 $2^3 + 2^3$

28 metres

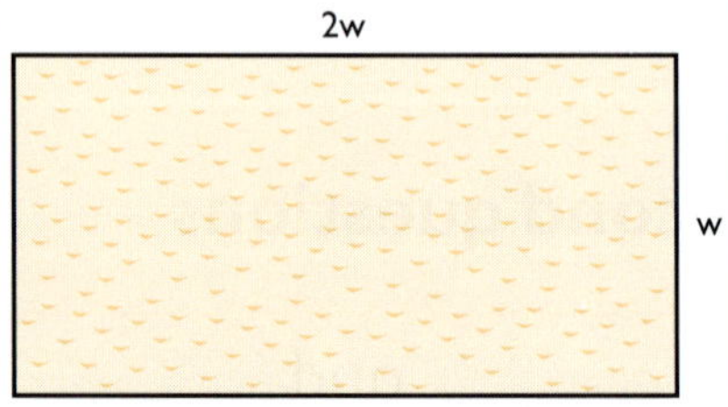

Perimeter = 18 metres

29

30 | $y - 4 = z$

1
1
1
1
1
1
1
1
1
1

TOTAL

10

Maths Test Answers

Paper 1

Question number	Answer	Mark	Comments and tips
Practice questions	208 795 28 42		You cannot use calculators for any of the questions in Paper 1. You can work answers out anywhere on the page or you can work answers out mentally. For some questions you might gain a mark for your written working out even if you get the answer wrong.
Calculations			
1(a – e)	100 6 128 60 48 1 mark for each	5	Always look at the finished equation when you have written a missing number to see if it makes sense. For the question ☐ – 50 = 78, if you incorrectly took away 50 from 78 and wrote the missing number 28, you can see that 28 – 50 doesn't equal 78!
Shape symmetry			
2	Shape B 0 2 Shape C 3 3 Shape D 0 1 Shape E 5 5 I mark is given for each shape.	4	A useful thing to remember is that for regular shapes (those with sides and angles the same size) the number of lines of symmetry and order of rotational symmetry are the same as the number of sides. Look at shapes A, C and E. They are regular shapes.
Canes			
3a	$\frac{3}{10}$	1	The line is divided into ten equal parts (the number on the bottom of your fraction) and the cane is as long as 3 parts (the number on the top).
3b	$\frac{3}{5}$	1	This question specifies giving your answer in its simplest form. Cane B is as long as six tenths. $\frac{6}{10} = \frac{3}{5}$ To simplify fractions, cancel the top and bottom numbers by the same number, in this case by 2.
3c	80%	1	Eight tenths as a percentage is 80%. If you think of the whole line as 100%, each part is one tenth (10%) so eight parts are 80%.
3d	40 cm	1	$\frac{2}{5}$ is the same value as four tenths. Four tenths of a metre is 40 cm.
3e	300 cm or 3 m	1	Ten pieces of cane A measuring 30 cm each would be 300 cm or 3 m.
3f	Cane E is longer than Cane B but shorter than Cane C.	1	$\frac{2}{3}$ of a metre is 66.6 cm. Cane B is 60 cm and Cane C is 80 cm.

Maths Test Answers

Question number	Answer	Mark	Comments and tips
School trip			
4a	£123 or £123.00	1	Note that amounts should never be written with both the **£** sign and a **p** sign, e.g. £123.00p.
4b	£600	1	
4c	£9.50	1	
4d	£11.52	1	To check an answer like this while sitting the paper, try adding the amount Leroy spends to the answer you have written. It should come to £20.
4e	£15.80	1	
Bags of money			
5a	$\frac{1}{12}$	1	There are 12 coins. The probability of picking the 1p coin is one out of twelve.
5b		1	The probability of picking a 20p coin is six out of twelve. This is the same as one half.
5c		1	There are 12 coins. The probability of picking a 5p coin is $\frac{2}{12}$ so the probability of not getting a 5p is $\frac{10}{12}$. Note that $\frac{10}{12}$ is the same as $\frac{5}{6}$
5d		1	The probability of picking a silver coin is $\frac{11}{12}$ as only the 1p is not silver.
5e	Your explanation should include the idea that tests are not always reliable. Davina only tried it 60 times. The probability of picking a 5p is still $\frac{2}{12}$ and the probability of picking a 10p is $\frac{3}{12}$.	1	The greater the number of tests carried out, the more likely the results will match the theoretical probability.
Fishy problems			
6a	$n + 4$	1	
6b	$n \div 2$ or $\frac{1}{2}n$ or $\frac{n}{2}$	1	Any of these three expressions are acceptable, but the second two are preferable.

Question number	Answer	Mark	Comments and tips
6c	$2n$	1	The answers $n \times 2$ or $2 \times n$ are acceptable, but it is better to shorten the expression to $2n$.
6d	$20n$	1	The answers $n \times 20$ or $20 \times n$ are acceptable, but it is better to shorten the expression to $20n$.
6e	The fish tanks do not hold the same amount. Your explanation should show that $3(n-3)$ becomes $3n-9$ when the brackets are removed.	1	When removing brackets you must multiply whatever is outside the brackets by <u>everything</u> inside the brackets. People sometimes forget and only multiply the first number in the brackets. $3(n-3)$ does NOT equal $3n-3$, but $3n-$ <u>**9**</u> .
Sequences			
7a	15 21 49 100 1 mark for each correct row.	2	The number of coloured squares is always 1 more than the shape number doubled. The number of white squares is always the shape number squared.
7b	$2n+1$ (or equivalent expression) n^2 or $n \times n$ 1 mark for each correct row.	2	The number of coloured squares is always 1 more than the shape number (n) doubled = $2n + 1$. The number of white squares is always the shape number squared: n^2.
7c	$n^2 + 2n + 1$	1	
7d	Set 2	1	A tip for finding the correct set in a question of this type is to look at the number multiplied by n, in this case 2. Look for the set of shapes which grows by 2 each time.
Angles			
8	$a = 50°$ $b = 30°$ $c = 150°$	3	Angle a is found by subtracting 130° from 180° (angles on a straight line). The angles inside a triangle add to 180°. The third angle is 20 (180 – 160) so 130 + 20 = 150, which means that b must be 30°. Angle c is found by subtracting b (30°) from 180°.
Linear equations			
9a	$y = 7$	1	Lines with the equation y = 'a number' are horizontal. Lines with the equation x = 'a number' are vertical. Lines with an equation with x and y are diagonal.

Question number	Answer	Mark	Comments and tips
9b	$y = x + 3$	1	In the general equation $y = mx + c$, m stands for the gradient. For this line, the gradient (slope) is the same as the line AB which is given as 1. The c stands for the point at which the line would cross the y axis. The line AB crosses at 7; the line you are finding, CD, would cross at 3.
9c	A diagonal line should be drawn, passing through the co-ordinates (0, 10) and (10, 0).	1	This equation can be rearranged to form the equation $x + y = 10$. You can see that if x is 0, $y = 10$ and when $x = 1$, $y = 9$ etc. These points can be plotted on the graph to form the line.
Areas			
10a	2 cm	2	Remember to look at the formula sheet at the beginning of the test to help you with questions of this type. 1 mark given for using the equation area = $\frac{(a + b)}{2} \times h$ even if answer is incorrect. The area of the parallelogram is 4.5 cm^2 so the area of the trapezium is therefore 13.5 cm^2. $13.5 = \frac{(4 + 9.5)}{2} \times h$ $13.5 = \frac{13.5}{2} \times h$ Here you can see that if 13.5 divided by 2 and multiplied by h is 13.5, h must be 2.
10b	Area = $12y^2$	1	Area = $\frac{(2y + 6y)}{2} \times 3y$ $= \frac{8y}{2} \times 3y \quad = 4y \times 3y \quad = 12y^2$

Maths Test Answers

Paper 2

Question number	Answer	Mark	Comments and tips
Running			
1a	26 40 14 40 58 18	2	Score 1 mark for each row. Each interval on the graph is worth 2 m.
1b	Your explanation should include the fact that Dev runs at quite a steady rate, whereas Ben starts more slowly and speeds up, but slows down again near the end.	2	
1c	Ben	1	You can see on the graph that Ben has reached the 60 m line.
Square sequences			
2a	Your explanation should show that you have noticed that the two central coloured squares in each shape are represented by $+2$ and the $3n$ represents the three 'legs' on each shape.	1	Notice that the number of coloured squares remains constant and the number of white squares grows. The parts that grow are represented in the expression by a number of n. The constant squares, such as the coloured ones, are represented by just a number.
2b	36 and 2	2	The rule is $3n + 2$. For shape 12, $n = 12$ so $3n + 1 = (3 \times 12) + 2 = 36$ and 2.
2c	20	1	The rule is $3n + 2$. If $3n + 2 = 62$, then $3n = 62 - 2 = 60$ If $3n = 60$, then n must be 20.
2d	$4n + 1$	1	There is 1 central coloured square (+1) and 4 'legs' ($4n$), so the total number is $4n + 1$. The equations $1 + 4n$ or $(4 \times n) + 1$ are also acceptable.
Cubes			
3a	A cuboid accurately drawn, e.g. 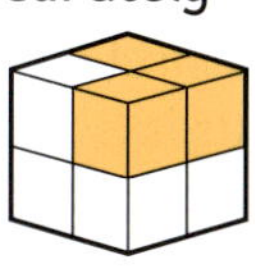 with 3 coloured cubes correctly positioned.	2	The cube can be drawn in a different orientation. 1 mark if coloured cubes are not correctly shaded.

Question number	Answer	Mark	Comments and tips
3b	2 cm, 2 cm, 2 cm	1	
3c	48 cm^3	2	The volume of a cuboid is found by multiplying the length by the width by the height: $3 \times 4 \times 4 = 48$ cm^3.
3d	4	1	
3e	$\frac{44}{48}$ or $\frac{22}{24}$ or $\frac{11}{12}$	1	If four cannot be seen then 44 (48 minus 4) can be seen. 44 out of a total of 48 is written as a fraction as $\frac{44}{48}$
Volume			
4	$x = 2.6$ cm	4	
Baking			
5a	100 g	1	The ratio is 2 parts butter for every 7 parts flour. We can write this as the ratio 2:7. If there is 350 g of flour (fifty times the number in the ratio) then butter must be fifty times the other number in the ratio, i.e. $2 \times 50 = 100$.
5b	280 g	1	The ratio is 2:7. If there is 80 g of butter (forty times the number in the ratio) then flour must be forty times the other number in the ratio, i.e. $7 \times 40 = 280$.
5c	1400 g flour and 400 g butter 1 mark each	2	In the ratio 2:7, there is a total of 9 parts. If a total of 1800 g is mixed (200 times the ratio total) then both butter and flour must be 200 times their numbers in the ratio.
Scalene triangle			
6a	To check your answer, measure the perpendicular height of your triangle. If the height is exactly 2.8 cm then you score 2 marks. If the answer is between 2.6 cm and 3 cm, you score 1 mark.	2	
6b	22° or 23°	1	
Area and circumference			
7a	200.96 cm^2 or 201 cm^2 Only 1 mark for the answer 201.06 cm^2 (use of π button on calculator)	2	Area of a circle = πr^2. The radius is half the diameter $(16 \div 2) = 8$ Area = $64 \times \pi = 64 \times 3.14$ NOTE: *If you have used the π button on your calculator your answer will be different. The question stated that π should be taken as 3.14.*

Question number	Answer	Mark	Comments and tips
7b	11 cm	2	The circumference of a circle is $2\pi r$ or πd. If the circumference is 69, then divide 69 by π to find the diameter and then halve to find r.
Sports day			
8a	110	1	Add together 2, 19, 38, 32, 15 and 5.
8b	This graph does not give enough information about the precise distances the students threw.	1	Within the distance 20–29, the students could have thrown over 25 m, in which case Serena is wrong, or under 25 m, in which case she is right.
8c	Again, we need more information.	1	The range of a set of data is found by subtracting the lowest value from the highest value.
8d	29.2 m 1 mark for 29.227 m or 29.23...	2	The total values for fx should be divided by 110 (the number of students) to find the mean value.
Money matters			
9	p = £4 q = £6 1 mark for each. 2 marks for these equations shown: $4p + 2 = 3q$ $8p - 2 = 5q$	4	There are different methods for solving simultaneous equations. One example is shown below: Double each value in the equation $4p + 2 = 3q$ to give $8p + 4 = 6q$. Subtract $8p - 2 = 5q$ from this equation to get $6 = q$, therefore Emily has £6. If $q = 6$, then $4p + 2 = 3 \times 6 = 18$. Thus $4p + 2 = 18$ and $4p = 16$, so p must be 4.
Field			
10	18 m 3 marks if your working shows the number 48.877 or 49, or a number with more than 2 digits, e.g. 18.12. Score 2 marks for the number 2389 in your working.	4	Let x be the length of the path. Use Pythagoras' Theorem ($a^2 + b^2 = c^2$). $42^2 + 25^2 = x^2$ so $x^2 = 2389$, therefore $x = 48.877$ m. Once the distance across the field has been found, add the distances 42 m and 25 m to get 67 m. This value is how far they walked. The difference between 67 m and 48.877 m is 18.123 m, which is 18 m to 2 significant figures.

Mental Maths Test

Answers

1. 0.75
2. 25
3. 60 000
4. 3000
5. $\frac{2}{3}$
6. 36.3
7. 2.5
8. 70%
9. 20 cm^2
10. 20
11. any two numbers that add to 8.32 e.g. 8.0 + 0.32
12. any fraction equivalent to five sixths e.g. $\frac{10}{12}$
13. 27 cm
14. 36
15. 13
16. 1.42
17. 24
18. any value larger than −3 and less than 2 e.g. −1
19. 4 and 9
20. 50
21. $\frac{3}{16}$
22. any three odd numbers that add to 33 e.g. 25, 5 and 3
23. 51.2
24. $4n$
25. £7.45
26. 19
27. $3^2 + 8$
28. 6 m
29. 8
30. $y - 2 = z + 2$

National Curriculum Levels

Write your scores below.

Mark scored in Paper 1		out of 45
Mark scored in Paper 2		out of 45
Mark scored in Mental Maths Test		out of 30
Total score		out of 120

Use this table to find what level you might be working at.

Mark	0 – 16	17 – 32	33 – 65	66 – 100	101 – 110	111 – 120
Level	**Level 3**	**Level 4**	**Level 5**	**Level 6**	**Level 7**	**Level 8**

If you need more practice in any Maths topics, use the WH Smith Key Stage 3 Maths Revision Guide.

English

English at Key Stage 3

In English pupils are required to sit two test papers:

Paper 1

Time allowed: 1 hour 30 minutes plus 15 minutes reading time

Section A – a test of reading based on a narrative or descriptive piece.

Section B – a test of reading based on an information text or on a poem.

Section C – a test of writing. Several options are given: writing a story, writing an argument or expressing a personal point of view.

Paper 2

Time allowed: 1 hour 15 minutes

This is based on the study of a Shakespeare play. For 2001 the choices are **Henry V, Twelfth Night** and **Macbeth**.

A booklet containing printed versions of scenes from the play is provided. A copy of the entire text is not permitted in the test.

Two questions are set on different scenes and each pupil must choose one of these for which to supply an answer.

Marking the papers

Each pupil is awarded a final score for the whole English test. This will equate to a National Curriculum level.

Paper 1

Section A is marked simply for the understanding of the passage set. This is judged by reading and writing tasks although the way in which the answers are written is not assessed.

Section B is marked for the ability to understand and describe an author's intention. Again, this is judged by reading and writing tasks although the way in which the answers are written is not assessed.

Section C is marked for the ability to write and communicate ideas. The style of writing does matter here as do the quality of ideas and grammatical features such as sentence structure, spelling, punctuation and grammar.

The mark scheme will vary from year to year for this paper but it will generally be worth about 60 marks .

Paper 2

This paper on a Shakespeare play is marked for:

- Understanding and Response – an understanding of Shakespeare's meaning and intention.
- Written Expression – an ability to write clearly using grammatical features such as sentence structure, spelling, punctuation and grammar.

The mark scheme will vary from year to year for this paper but it will generally be worth about 40 marks.

Teachers, who know each pupil well, also give their assessment of coursework produced throughout Key Stage 3. They also provide a Speaking and Listening assessment which cannot be assessed in written tests.

Tips for success at Key Stage 3

- Look at the entire test paper first to establish what has to be done. Highlight the time restraints and the number of questions which need to be answered.
- Pace yourself – keep an eye on the clock.
- Read the questions carefully. Underline key words, e.g. 'compare', 'two reasons…' Be relevant in your answers.
- Avoid getting too involved with any one question. You may have a great deal to say about it, but it will only be worth a set number of marks.
- Follow the help given on the paper. If the examiners have given a list of points to follow then use these as the plan for your work.
- Make notes on the test paper. Underline important points and circle or highlight information relevant to the question.
- Back up any points you make with short quotations from the passage.
- If you get stuck on a question, leave it for the moment – but remember to leave a page empty in your answer book in case you want to go back.
- Your basic English is important – you need to communicate what you know and understand. Look carefully for those words you often spell incorrectly!
- If you have time left, go back over your answers.

Setting the test – notes for parents

The tests in this book are modelled as closely as possible on the 'real thing' so pupils will not be surprised by the test format. However, parents can help with the pressure of the tests by using the material in this book as a resource for teaching and learning. Do not just sit a pupil down with the test and tell him or her to 'get on with it'; share the experiences, questions and discussion that arises from the tests. Try sitting one yourself!

- Talk about each of the questions and possible ways forward. At this stage, discussion will be more useful than writing.
- Choose a comfortable environment in which to do the tests together.
- Mark the work together, praising positive points as well as pointing out things which are not correct.
- Look closely at how incorrect responses can be corrected, what needs to be learned or changed and how this can be done realistically. It is useful to list just two or three things which need to be done or learned before the next test session.
- Stick to the time limits – but do not insist that the entire test paper has to be completed at one go.
- Give immediate feedback – do not wait too long to discuss the performance of the candidate.
- Be positive about achievements!
- If you have any questions, ask a teacher.

Marking the test

Page 77 shows how the marks for this test are correlated.

Shakespeare

Preparing for the Shakespeare Paper

There is only one way to prepare for answering questions on a Shakespeare play – read the play! Watching the video is not good enough! Shakespeare plays are not easy for us, mostly because of their language, but going to see one at the theatre will prove that they are really easy to understand as the characters think and behave in exactly the same ways as people today.

In your test, you will be asked to deal with one aspect of the play you have studied in relation to one or two scenes, but you must also be prepared to share your knowledge of the rest of the play by putting certain aspects of the play into context and saying what has happened before – and if anything has changed – and even what will happen later in the play.

The questions in this book give you a flavour of the kinds of questions you could find in your final tests. You will have dealt with most aspects of the play in school – character, plot, Shakespeare's language. Even if the question in front of you on the day looks different from any question you have dealt with in school, don't panic! You will have the information you need if you stop to think. This section of your assessment differs from the other because you can prepare for this. You know what you will get to a certain extent. You will not be allowed to take the text into the test; you need to rely on your memory and understanding of the work you have done in Year 9.

Remember: Do not write everything you know about the play – you are not being tested on how good your memory is and answer the question you have been set – not the one you wish had been set!

Draft your answer before you finally write it:

- Take time to think about what information you need from the scene printed for you.
- Spend at least 15 minutes carefully reading the scene you have chosen.
- Do not be afraid to underline or circle important quotations. Write notes in the margin as you go along.
- Use the helpful pointers given to you on the question paper and write notes on each section. Prove each of your points with a brief quotation.
- Take each of the pointers in turn and think about how to join them together as paragraphs later on. You could even number them in your notes to ensure that you do not miss any out.
- Do not write out huge sections from the play. The examiner wants to know what and how you write – not how Shakespeare did!

It is important that you pace yourself effectively. You have time to read and annotate the scene printed for you and time to draft and write your answer. You will not be given extra time.

You are being assessed in this section on your knowledge and awareness of the Shakespeare play you have studied – its plot, ideas, the characters and why they behave in the way that they do, the language and even the staging of the scene. But remember, you will also have to write clearly to communicate these ideas. Hence marks are allocated for use of appropriate style, clarity and organisation of writing, spelling, grammar and punctuation. Your handwriting is also important, so leave enough time to check your work.

Checklist of important features in your answer

Features to consider	Yes	No
Paragraphs Is my work divided into paragraphs so that the examiner can see when I stop writing about one aspect and start writing about another?		
Quotations Are my quotations too long? Have I used quotation marks? Have I started long quotations on a new line? Have I written my quotations on lines as in the text? Have I introduced my quotations by using a colon (:)?		
Style Is my writing too chatty? Am I writing in an appropriate style? Have I written in complete sentences? Is my handwriting clear and neat?		
Length The answer booklet you are given is A4 in size. Have I written between 3 and 4 sides on paper for my answer? If you use any pages for planning, just draw a line through this.		

Marking your tests

Your work on a Shakespeare play will be considered from two points of view:

- **Understanding and Response:** the content of what you write – how you have understood and responded to Shakespeare and his ideas, how his characters behave and why they do, the development and changes in the plot and his language.
- **Written Expression:** the way you write – your choice of appropriate style, your use of paragraphs, vocabulary, punctuation and spelling as well as your ability to write clearly and legibly.

To achieve the highest grades you will need to:

- Know and understand your Shakespeare play well
- Write clearly and to the point – do not ramble on, giving irrelevant information from the play just because you know it
- Answer the question you have been set in an organised way
- Write from a personal point of view so that the examiner gets a sense of what you think and feel – not just what your teacher said
- Write accurately in clear, well-punctuated English, using well-constructed sentences.

English Test

Paper 1

- At the beginning of this test, you have 15 minutes to read the paper and make notes but you must not start to write your answers until you are told to.
- Then you have 1 hour and 30 minutes to write your answers.
- You should answer **ALL** the questions in Sections A and B.
- Then choose **ONE** question only from Section C.
- You should spend about: 20 minutes on question 1
  10 minutes on question 2
  20 minutes on question 3
  35 minutes on question 4
  5 minutes checking your work.
- Check your work carefully.

N.B.
Do not be afraid to underline or circle or highlight the key points in the texts as you are reading them. You can write in the margin too.

Read the following passage.
Then answer question 1 and question 2.

The passage comes from Dylan Thomas' autobiography and tells of a visit to his grandfather's.

In the middle of the night I woke from a dream full of whips, lariats as long as serpents, and runaway coaches on mountain passes, and wide, windy gallops over cactus fields, and I heard the old man in the next room crying, 'Gee-up!' and 'Whoa!' and trotting his tongue on the roof of his mouth.

It was the first time I had stayed in grandpa's house. The floorboards had creaked like mice as I climbed into bed, and the mice between the walls had creaked like wood as though another visitor was walking on them. It was a mild summer night, but curtains had flapped and branches beaten against the window. I had pulled the sheets over my head, and soon was roaring and riding in a book.

'Whoa there, my beauties!' cried grandpa. His voice sounded very young and loud, and his tongue had powerful hooves, and he made his bedroom into a great meadow. I thought I would see if he was ill, or had set the bedclothes on fire, for my mother had said that he lit his pipe under the blankets, and had warned me to run to his help if I smelt smoke in the night. I went on tiptoe through the darkness to his bedroom door, brushing against the furniture and upsetting a candlestick with a thump. When I saw there was a light in the room I felt frightened, and as I opened the door I heard grandpa shout, 'Gee-up!' as loudly as a bull with a megaphone.

He was sitting straight up in bed and rocking from side to side as though the bed were on a rough road; the knotted edges of the counterpane were his reins; his invisible horses stood in a shadow beyond the bedside candle. Over a white flannel nightshirt he was wearing a red waistcoat with walnut-size brass buttons. The over-filled bowl of his pipe smouldered among his whiskers like a little burning hayrick on a stick. At the sight of me his hands dropped from the reins and lay blue and quiet, the bed stopped still on a level road, he muffled his tongue into silence, and the horses drew softly up.

'Is there anything the matter, grandpa?' I asked, though the clothes were not on fire. His face in the candlelight looked like a ragged quilt pinned upright on the black air and patched all over with goat-beards.

He stared at me mildly. Then he blew down his pipe, scattering the sparks and making a high, wet dog-whistle of the stem, and shouted: 'Ask no questions.'

After a pause, he said slyly: 'Do you ever have nightmares, boy?'

I said: 'No.'

'Oh, yes, you do,' he said.

I said I was woken by a voice that was shouting to horses.

'What did I tell you?' he said. 'You eat too much. Who ever heard of horses in a bedroom?'

He fumbled under his pillow, brought out a small, tinkling bag, and carefully untied its strings. He put a sovereign in my hand, and said: 'Buy a cake.' I thanked him and wished him goodnight.

As I closed my bedroom door, I heard his voice crying loudly and gaily, 'Gee-up! Gee-up!' And the rocking of the travelling bed.

Question 1 10 marks in total

Show how the author (Dylan Thomas) effectively creates the old man's fantasy.

In your answer you should concentrate on:

- The changing attitude of the boy towards his grandfather.
- How the boy becomes aware of what is happening and what he had been doing previously.
- What the house is like.
- What he hears and sees as he gets closer to the room.
- What the grandfather's fantasy is and how the old man is dramatising this.
- The unusual images and description used by the writer.

Refer to words or phrases in the passage to support your ideas.

Question 2 8 marks in total

Write about what you learn about the character of the old man and how he explains what he is doing.

In your answer you should comment on:

- What his fantasy consists of and how you feel about this.
- How the grandfather acts out his fantasy and your reaction to this.
- How the grandfather reacts when he first sees the boy.
- How he explains his behaviour.
- How he convinces the boy he has not witnessed the scene.

Refer to words or phrases in the passage to support your ideas.

Read the poem below.
Then answer question 3.

Warning

When I am an old woman I shall wear purple
With a red hat which doesn't go and doesn't suit me,
And I shall spend my pension on brandy and summer gloves
And satin sandals and say we've no money for butter.
I shall sit down on the pavement when I'm tired
And gobble up samples in shops and press alarm bells
And run my stick along the public railings
And make up for the sobriety* of my youth.
I shall go out in my slippers in the rain
And pick the flowers in other people's gardens
And learn to spit.

You can wear terrible shirts and grow more fat
And eat three pounds of sausages at a go
Or only bread and pickle for a week
And hoard pens and pencils and beermats and things in boxes.

But now we must have clothes that keep us dry
And pay our rent and not swear in the street
And set a good example for the children.
We will have friends to dinner and read the papers.
But maybe I ought to practise a little now?
So people who know me are not too shocked and surprised
When suddenly I am old and wear purple.

Jenny Joseph
* sobriety = self-control

Question 3 10 marks in total

a) The definition of someone who is 'eccentric' is: 'not following the established pattern of conduct; odd'. Explain whether you think the woman in this poem deserves this description.
6 marks

In your answer you should comment on:

- What you expect the established 'pattern of conduct' might be for a woman such as the one in the poem.
- What she would like to do and why.
- How you feel about this.

Refer to words and phrases in the poem to support your ideas.

b) Explain how the poet contrasts what people expect of an old woman with how she would like to behave.
4 marks

In your answer you should comment on:

- What the poem says in the final section about what is expected.
- How the earlier images contrast with this.
- How the woman feels about this.
- How the reader feels about this.

Refer to words and phrases in the poem to support your ideas.

This section of the paper is a test of writing. You will be assessed on:

- Your ideas and the way you organise them.
- Your ability to write clearly, using paragraphs and accurate grammar, spelling and punctuation.

Choose ONE of the following:

Question 4 32 marks in total

EITHER

a) Write an account of an embarrassing moment when you were caught acting out of character. How did you explain your behaviour?

In your answer you should:

- Use descriptive language and imagery to make the experience as real as possible to your reader.

OR

b) Imagine you are the woman in the poem. Write about some occasions when she behaved in these ways, including the effects of her behaviour.

In your answer you should:

- Write about no more than two or three occasions.
- Focus on describing what actually happened in as much detail as possible.
- Consider how people around might react: what they would say, think and do.

OR

c) Some say that respect for the older generation is disappearing. Write a newspaper article about this, suggesting ways of changing the attitudes of young people.

In your answer you should:

- Write in an appropriate journalistic style.
- Give your views with evidence or stories to back this up.
- Provide a few sensible and developed strategies for change.

Henry V

If you have studied **Henry V** do this task.

Time allowed: 75 minutes
Your work will be assessed for your knowledge and understanding of the play and the way you express your ideas.
Check your work carefully.

Henry V
From Act 2 Scene 2

Task

- Show how this scene reveals a change in Henry – from the 'madcap' Prince of his youth, to a serious, mature politician fit to rule a nation.

Before you write you should think about:

- What the aristocracy used to think of Henry because of his previous lifestyle in the taverns with Falstaff and his crew.
- How the king behaved to the traitors in the first part of the scene.
- How Henry allows them to trap themselves by stating their own views which he later uses against them.
- How Henry knows about the traitors and what this shows about him.
- How the king uses irony in the scene and how his tone changes when the traitors are revealed.
- How the final part of the scene gives us an indication of what Henry will do in France.

Read the task again before you begin to write your answer.

EXAMINER'S TIPS

Remind yourself about some of the following points:

- Set the scene in the context of the rest of the play. Henry was once seen as a 'madcap Prince'. He filled his hours with 'riots, banquets, sports'.
- Now that he is king he needs to take responsibility for his actions, as now he is responsible for the nation – 'The king is full of grace and fair regard'.
- The scene with the French Ambassador and the gift of tennis balls has shown us his capability: 'Tell him he hath made a match with such a wrangler'
- Henry knows the men are traitors. He cleverly plays along with them until they provide their own punishment.
- This is a mature king, a clever and manipulative politician. He is 'his own man' and the passion of his words shows his patriotism.
- His final speech echoes his feelings and passion – as well as his humanity – at Agincourt.

Henry V
From Act 2 Scene 2

Southampton, a council chamber

GREY
Sir,
You show great mercy, if you give him life,
After the taste of much correction.

KING HENRY V
Alas, your too much love and care of me
Are heavy orisons 'gainst this poor wretch!
If little faults, proceeding on distemper,
Shall not be wink'd at, how shall we stretch our eye
When capital crimes, chew'd, swallow'd and digested,
Appear before us? We'll yet enlarge that man,
Though Cambridge, Scroop and Grey, in their dear care
And tender preservation of our person,
Would have him punished. And now to our French causes:
Who are the late commissioners?

CAMBRIDGE
I one, my lord:
Your highness bade me ask for it to-day.

SCROOP)
So did you me, my liege.
GREY)
And I, my royal sovereign.

KING HENRY V
Then, Richard Earl of Cambridge, there is yours;
There yours, Lord Scroop of Masham; and, sir knight,
Grey of Northumberland, this same is yours:
Read them; and know, I know your worthiness.
My Lord of Westmoreland, and uncle Exeter,
We will aboard to night. Why, how now, gentlemen!
What see you in those papers that you lose
So much complexion? Look ye, how they change!
Their cheeks are paper. Why, what read you there
That hath so cowarded and chased your blood
Out of appearance?

CAMBRIDGE
I do confess my fault;
And do submit me to your highness' mercy.

GREY

SCROOP
To which we all appeal.

KING HENRY V
The mercy that was quick in us but late,
By your own counsel is suppress'd and kill'd:
You must not dare, for shame, to talk of mercy;
For your own reasons turn into your bosoms,
As dogs upon their masters, worrying you.
ee you, my princes, and my noble peers,
These English monsters! My Lord of Cambridge here,
You know how apt our love was to accord
To furnish him with all appertinents
Belonging to his honour; and this man
Hath, for a few light crowns, lightly conspired,
And sworn unto the practices of France,

To kill us here in Hampton: to the which
This knight, no less for bounty bound to us
Than Cambridge is, hath likewise sworn. But, O,
What shall I say to thee, Lord Scroop? thou cruel,
Ingrateful, savage and inhuman creature!
Thou that didst bear the key of all my counsels,
That knew'st the very bottom of my soul,
That almost mightst have coin'd me into gold,
Wouldst thou have practised on me for thy use,
May it be possible, that foreign hire
Could out of thee extract one spark of evil
That might annoy my finger? 'tis so strange,
That, though the truth of it stands off as gross
As black and white, my eye will scarcely see it.
Treason and murder ever kept together,
As two yoke-devils sworn to either's purpose,
Working so grossly in a natural cause,
That admiration did not whoop at them:
But thou, 'gainst all proportion, didst bring in
Wonder to wait on treason and on murder:
And whatsoever cunning fiend it was
That wrought upon thee so preposterously
Hath got the voice in hell for excellence:
All other devils that suggest by treasons
Do botch and bungle up damnation
With patches, colours, and with forms being fetch'd
From glistering semblances of piety;
But he that temper'd thee bade thee stand up,
Gave thee no instance why thou shouldst do treason,
Unless to dub thee with the name of traitor.
If that same demon that hath gull'd thee thus
Should with his lion gait walk the whole world,
He might return to vasty Tartar back,
And tell the legions 'I can never win
A soul so easy as that Englishman's.'
O, how hast thou with 'jealousy infected
The sweetness of affiance! Show men dutiful?
Why, so didst thou: seem they grave and learned?
Why, so didst thou: come they of noble family?
Why, so didst thou: seem they religious?
Why, so didst thou: or are they spare in diet,
Free from gross passion or of mirth or anger,
Constant in spirit, not swerving with the blood,
Garnish'd and deck'd in modest complement,
Not working with the eye without the ear,
And but in purged judgment trusting neither?
Such and so finely bolted didst thou seem:
And thus thy fall hath left a kind of blot,
To mark the full-fraught man and best indued
With some suspicion. I will weep for thee;
For this revolt of thine, methinks, is like
Another fall of man. Their faults are open:
Arrest them to the answer of the law;
And God acquit them of their practices!

EXETER
I arrest thee of high treason, by the name of
Richard Earl of Cambridge.
I arrest thee of high treason, by the name of
Henry Lord Scroop of Masham.
I arrest thee of high treason, by the name of
Thomas Grey, knight, of Northumberland.

SCROOP
Our purposes God justly hath discover'd;
And I repent my fault more than my death;
Which I beseech your highness to forgive,
Although my body pay the price of it.

CAMBRIDGE
For me, the gold of France did not seduce;
Although I did admit it as a motive
The sooner to effect what I intended:
But God be thanked for prevention;
Which I in sufferance heartily will rejoice,
Beseeching God and you to pardon me.

GREY
Never did faithful subject more rejoice
At the discovery of most dangerous treason
Than I do at this hour joy o'er myself.
Prevented from a damned enterprise:
My fault, but not my body, pardon, sovereign.

KING HENRY V
God quit you in his mercy! Hear your sentence.
You have conspired against our royal person,
Join'd with an enemy proclaim'd and from his coffers
Received the golden earnest of our death;
Wherein you would have sold your king to slaughter,
His princes and his peers to servitude,
His subjects to oppression and contempt
And his whole kingdom into desolation.
Touching our person seek we no revenge;
But we our kingdom's safety must so tender,
Whose ruin you have sought, that to her laws
We do deliver you. Get you therefore hence,
Poor miserable wretches, to your death:
The taste whereof, God of his mercy give
You patience to endure, and true repentance
Of all your dear offences! Bear them hence.

[Exeunt CAMBRIDGE, SCROOP and GREY, guarded]

Now, lords, for France; the enterprise whereof
Shall be to you, as us, like glorious.
We doubt not of a fair and lucky war,
Since God so graciously hath brought to light
This dangerous treason lurking in our way
To hinder our beginnings. We doubt not now
But every rub is smoothed on our way.
Then forth, dear countrymen: let us deliver
Our puissance into the hand of God,
Putting it straight in expedition.
Cheerly to sea; the signs of war advance:
No king of England, if not king of France.

[Exeunt]

Twelfth Night

If you have studied **Twelfth Night** do this task.

Time allowed: 75 minutes

Your work will be assessed for your knowledge and understanding of the play and the way you express your ideas.

Check your work carefully.

Twelfth Night
From Act 3 Scene 4

Task
- Imagine you are going to direct this scene for a class performance.
- Explain how you will want the pupils acting the parts to show the true motivations of the comic characters, but also to bring out the serious nature of the themes of the play.

Before you begin to write you should think about:

- The themes of the play are confusion caused by disguise and the many-faceted nature of love.
- The scene is comic because of the confusion and the stupidity of many of the characters acting out of context. It is also serious because the comedy results in injury and cruel actions. People very much take advantage of others' shortcomings.
- Sir Toby uses the stupid Sir Andrew. Malvolio is 'sick of self love' and deludes himself. Olivia is tricked by disguise into a futile relationship.

Read the task again before you begin to write your answer.

EXAMINER'S TIPS

Remind yourself about some of the following points:

- Set the scene in the context of the rest of the play. This scene shows the audience how the confusion caused by disguise can be painful as well as amusing. At the beginning of the scene, Olivia loves Cesario, who is in fact Viola, in disguise.
- Malvolio has been tricked by the other comic characters for spoiling their fun one evening – 'shall there be no more cakes and ale?' – into thinking Olivia loves him, and he has changed his character and reactions. He is dressed in yellow stockings, cross-gartered and his speech 'some achieve greatness ...' mystifies Olivia. She is told he is mad and he will be locked away – 'in a dark room and bound'. This is amusing, but also cruel.
- Meanwhile Sir Toby is playing a trick on Sir Andrew by getting him to challenge the youth Cesario – in competition for the love of Olivia.
- They are both cowards but when Sir Andrew strikes the person he thinks is the boy, he strikes Viola's brother. The comedy arises from confusion.

Twelfth Night
From Act 3 Scene 4

SIR TOBY BELCH	Prithee, hold thy peace; this is not the way: do you not see you move him? let me alone with him.
FABIAN	No way but gentleness; gently, gently: the fiend is rough, and will not be roughly used.
SIR TOBY BELCH	Why, how now, my bawcock! how dost thou, chuck?
MALVOLIO	Sir!
SIR TOBY BELCH	Ay, Biddy, come with me. What, man! 'tis not for gravity to play at cherry-pit with Satan: hang him, foul collier!
MARIA	Get him to say his prayers, good Sir Toby, get him to pray.
MALVOLIO	My prayers, minx!
MARIA	No, I warrant you, he will not hear of godliness.
MALVOLIO	Go, hang yourselves all! you are idle shallow things: I am not of your element: you shall know more hereafter. [Exit]
SIR TOBY BELCH	Is't possible?
FABIAN	If this were played upon a stage now, I could condemn it as an improbable fiction.
SIR TOBY BELCH	His very genius hath taken the infection of the device, man.
MARIA	Nay, pursue him now, lest the device take air and taint.
FABIAN	Why, we shall make him mad indeed.
MARIA	The house will be the quieter.
SIR TOBY BELCH	Come, we'll have him in a dark room and bound. My niece is already in the belief that he's mad: we may carry it thus, for our pleasure and his penance, till our very pastime, tired out of breath, prompt us to have mercy on him: at which time we will bring the device to the bar and crown thee for a finder of madmen. But see, but see.
	[Enter SIR ANDREW]
FABIAN	More matter for a May morning.
SIR ANDREW	Here's the challenge, read it: I warrant there's vinegar and pepper in't.
FABIAN	Is't so saucy?
SIR ANDREW	Ay, is't, I warrant him: do but read.
SIR TOBY BELCH	Give me. [Reads] 'Youth, whatsoever thou art, thou art but a scurvy fellow.'
FABIAN	Good, and valiant.

SIR TOBY BELCH	[Reads] 'Wonder not, nor admire not in thy mind, why I do call thee so, for I will show thee no reason for't.'
FABIAN	A good note; that keeps you from the blow of the law.
SIR TOBY BELCH	[Reads] 'Thou comest to the lady Olivia, and in my sight she uses thee kindly: but thou liest in thy throat; that is not the matter I challenge thee for.'
FABIAN	Very brief, and to exceeding good sense-less.
SIR TOBY BELCH	[Reads] 'I will waylay thee going home; where if it be thy chance to kill me,'—
FABIAN	Good.
SIR TOBY BELCH	[Reads] 'Thou killest me like a rogue and a villain.'
FABIAN	Still you keep o' the windy side of the law: good.
SIR TOBY BELCH	[Reads] 'Fare thee well; and God have mercy upon one of our souls! He may have mercy upon mine; but my hope is better, and so look to thyself. Thy friend, as thou usest him, and thy sworn enemy, ANDREW AGUECHEEK. If this letter move him not, his legs cannot: I'll give't him.
MARIA	You may have very fit occasion for't: he is now in some commerce with my lady, and will by and by depart.
SIR TOBY BELCH	Go, Sir Andrew: scout me for him at the corner of the orchard like a bum-baily: so soon as ever thou seest him, draw; and, as thou drawest, swear horrible; for it comes to pass oft that a terrible oath, with a swaggering accent sharply twanged off, gives manhood more approbation than ever proof itself would have earned him. Away!
SIR ANDREW	Nay, let me alone for swearing. [Exit]
SIR TOBY BELCH	Now will not I deliver his letter: for the behaviour of the young gentleman gives him out to be of good capacity and breeding; his employment between his lord and my niece confirms no less: therefore this letter, being so excellently ignorant, will breed no terror in the youth: he will find it comes from a clodpole. But, sir, I will deliver his challenge by word of mouth; set upon Aguecheek a notable report of valour; and drive the gentleman, as I know his youth will aptly receive it, into a most hideous opinion of his rage, skill, fury and impetuosity. This will so fright them both that they will kill one another by the look, like cockatrices.
	[Re-enter OLIVIA, with VIOLA]
FABIAN	Here he comes with your niece: give them way till he take leave, and presently after him.
SIR TOBY BELCH	I will meditate the while upon some horrid message for a challenge.

Macbeth

If you have studied **Macbeth** do this task.

Time allowed: 75 minutes

Your work will be assessed for your knowledge and understanding of the play and the way you express your ideas.

Check your work carefully.

Macbeth
Act 2 Scene 1

Task
- Use this scene to discuss how the prophecies of the three witches change the lives of Macbeth and Banquo and how their relationship changes throughout the play.

Before you begin to write you should think about:

- The first prophecies of the three witches given to Macbeth
- The prophecies given to Banquo and the effect of them on Macbeth.
- What Macbeth does to reach his goals and how this leads to even more evil deeds.
- Why Macbeth sees Banquo as a threat and what he does about this.
- How he receives more prophecies from the witches and what they really mean.
- How Macbeth becomes a very different person by the end of the play.

Read the task again before you begin to write your answer.

EXAMINER'S TIPS

Remind yourself about some of the following points:

- Set the scene in the context of the rest of the play. Macbeth and Banquo meet the three witches coming back victorious from battle: ' brave Macbeth – well he deserves that name'.
- They give him three apparently impossible prophecies, but when two come true in quick succession, Macbeth believes he can become 'king hereafter'. The only problem is that he will have to kill the king.
- Banquo is told he will 'get kings, though thou be none' and Macbeth realises he is a threat to his own security on the throne.
- This scene takes place in Macbeth's castle when the King is staying there. Macbeth knows he is about to murder Duncan and the conversation between these two old 'friends' is heavily ironic. 'I think not of them.'
- Macbeth needs to murder and continue murdering to secure his position: 'It will have blood, they say; blood will have blood.' Banquo is murdered, Macduff's wife and children are murdered; Fleance, however, escapes and this tortures Macbeth: 'to be thus is nothing;/But to be safely thus ...'
- When Macbeth returns to the witches, he is deluded by their new prophecies into thinking himself invincible, but at the end he is left alone as 'a tyrant' and he begins 'to grow aweary of this world.' He realises he has lost all –including his friendship – because of his 'vaulting ambition which o'erleaps itself/And falls on the other.'

Macbeth
Act 2 Scene 1

Court of Macbeth's castle.

[Enter BANQUO, and FLEANCE bearing a torch before him]

BANQUO How goes the night, boy?

FLEANCE The moon is down; I have not heard the clock.

BANQUO And she goes down at twelve.

FLEANCE I take't, 'tis later, sir.

BANQUO Hold, take my sword. There's husbandry in heaven;
Their candles are all out. Take thee that too.
A heavy summons lies like lead upon me,
And yet I would not sleep: merciful powers,
Restrain in me the cursed thoughts that nature
Gives way to in repose!

Act 1, Scene 2

[Enter MACBETH, and a Servant with a torch]

Give me my sword.
Who's there?

MACBETH A friend.

BANQUO What, sir, not yet at rest? The king's a-bed:
He hath been in unusual pleasure, and
Sent forth great largess to your offices.
This diamond he greets your wife withal,
By the name of most kind hostess; and shut up
In measureless content.

MACBETH Being unprepared,
Our will became the servant to defect;
Which else should free have wrought.

BANQUO All's well.
I dreamt last night of the three weird sisters:
To you they have show'd some truth.

MACBETH I think not of them:
Yet, when we can entreat an hour to serve,
We would spend it in some words upon that business,
If you would grant the time.

BANQUO At your kind'st leisure.

MACBETH If you shall cleave to my consent, when 'tis,
It shall make honour for you.

BANQUO So I lose none
In seeking to augment it, but still keep
My bosom franchised and allegiance clear,
I shall be counsell'd.

MACBETH Good repose the while!

BANQUO Thanks, sir: the like to you!

[Exeunt BANQUO and FLEANCE]

MACBETH Go bid thy mistress, when my drink is ready,
She strike upon the bell. Get thee to bed.

[Exit Servant]

Is this a dagger which I see before me,
The handle toward my hand? Come, let me clutch thee.
I have thee not, and yet I see thee still.
Art thou not, fatal vision, sensible
To feeling as to sight? or art thou but
A dagger of the mind, a false creation,
Proceeding from the heat-oppressed brain?
I see thee yet, in form as palpable
As this which now I draw.
Thou marshall'st me the way that I was going;
And such an instrument I was to use.
Mine eyes are made the fools o' the other senses,
Or else worth all the rest; I see thee still,
And on thy blade and dudgeon gouts of blood,
Which was not so before. There's no such thing:
It is the bloody business which informs
Thus to mine eyes. Now o'er the one halfworld
Nature seems dead, and wicked dreams abuse
The curtain'd sleep; witchcraft celebrates
Pale Hecate's offerings, and wither'd murder,
Alarum'd by his sentinel, the wolf,
Whose howl's his watch, thus with his stealthy pace.
With Tarquin's ravishing strides, towards his design
Moves like a ghost. Thou sure and firm-set earth,
Hear not my steps, which way they walk, for fear
Thy very stones prate of my whereabout,
And take the present horror from the time,
Which now suits with it. Whiles I threat, he lives:
Words to the heat of deeds too cold breath gives.

[A bell rings]

I go, and it is done; the bell invites me.
Hear it not, Duncan; for it is a knell
That summons thee to heaven or to hell.

[Exit]

English Test Answers

Paper 1

It is difficult to mark answers in an English test because there is often not a 'right answer' as there could be in Maths. The questions are often open to interpretation. Examiners for the English paper do not have a rigid mark scheme, but they will have a core of important points which will need to be covered to achieve a particular score.

A mark scheme is provided for each question. You will need to judge how well the points made in the answer match with the score criteria. Any point should be clearly stated.

Question 1 10 marks in total

Show how the author (Dylan Thomas) effectively creates the old man's fantasy.

In your answer you should concentrate on:

- The boy has been told that his grandfather is somewhat of a 'danger' – he might set the house alight because he smokes in bed. There is also a suggestion that he 'might be ill'. This gives us an impression that he is old and frail. The author obviously feels that he is somewhat eccentric – he is even a little afraid of the man: 'I felt frightened'. As a child he seems to accept the eccentric behaviour of the old man – the cowboy game the old man is playing is one that a young boy might play as well.
- The boy has been reading cowboy stories and has fallen asleep: 'I woke from a dream full of whips… windy gallops over cactus fields… roaring and riding in a book.' When he is awoken by his grandfather's noises he still thinks he is dreaming. He hears 'trotting the tongue on the roof of his mouth' – making noises like a galloping horse and other 'cowboy' noises. He sees a light under the door when he goes to investigate.
- The boy is already somewhat afraid of the old, eccentric house. The imagery is of creaking and 'branches beaten against the window'. He sets off in the darkness and knocks against the furniture.
- When he opens the door his grandfather makes his final 'Gee-up' noise. He has been caught imagining that he is riding a wagon or a horse – 'the counterpane… his reins.' His grandfather is wearing a red waistcoat and is smoking a pipe. The old man does not stop suddenly because he has been 'caught'. He 'muffled his tongue into silence and the horses drew softly up'. He continues with the fantasy as if there is nothing wrong. He then moves through the complicated procedure of persuading the boy that he has been dreaming the whole event, but gives him some money as a bribe. As the boy leaves, the old man continues with his fantasy.
- The writer makes the scene unusual by his use of imagery and description. He changes words into unusual verbs: 'trotting his tongue on the roof of his mouth'. The noises are described in two ways – the floorboards as mice; the mice as floorboards. The old man's tongue is animated: 'his tongue had powerful hooves'. Some of the metaphors and similes are very unusual: 'his bedroom … a great meadow', 'as loudly as a bull with a megaphone', 'like a little burning hayrick on a stick'.

2 marks per point made fully.

Score	National Curriculum Level	
9 or 10	Level 7+	Exceptional answer
7 or 8	Level 7	Well above average answer
5 or 6	Level 6	Above average answer
3 or 4	Level 5	Average or below average answer
1 or 2	Level 4 or below	Well below average answer

Question 2 8 marks in total

Write about what you learn about the character of the old man and how he explains what he is doing.

In your answer you should comment on:

- The fantasy of the old man goes back to a scene in the Wild West. He imagines he is riding a wagon down 'a rough road'. He is dressed for the part and is totally absorbed by this activity. This seems very eccentric for an adult but some may feel that it is acceptable for an old person. Others may feel it is unacceptable for any adult. This gives us the impression of an old man who is perhaps senile; indeed, the boy has been told to look after him because he may not be able to look after himself.
- However, the old man is in fact in control of all that he is doing. He is not shocked by the child's entry. He slowly stops and does not try to hide what he was doing. This would cause more attention to be drawn to him. He has a firm understanding of young children – that they may be easily influenced not only by what an adult tells them but also by bribery.
- The boy does not really comprehend what is happening at first: 'Is there anything the matter, Grandpa?' The image he uses of the 'ragged quilt' makes the old man seem even more sympathetic. However the man's strategy is very clever. He persuades the child he is having a dream. Some may feel he is a devious or sly character, but his argument is a clever one: 'Do you ever have nightmares, boy?' He is in fact making a joke of it ('mares' are female horses) so he is enjoying the activity of getting out of the situation. Finally the old man bribes the child with money: 'Buy a cake'.
- He is not embarrassed by being 'caught': as soon as the boy goes, he continues with his fantasy.

2 marks per point made fully.

Score	National Curriculum Level	
8	Level 7+	Exceptional answer
6 or 7	Level 7	Well above average answer
5	Level 6	Above average answer
3 or 4	Level 5	Average or below average answer
1 or 2	Level 4 or below	Well below average answer

Question 3 10 marks in total

c) The definition of someone who is 'eccentric' is: 'not following the established pattern of conduct; odd'. Explain whether you think the woman in this poem deserves this description.
6 marks

In your answer you should comment on:

- The interest in the poem lies in the fact that the narrator can fantasise about what it might be like to offend all the conventions of society. We do not know whether she will actually do any of these 'shocking' things, but they appeal to our sense of the absurd. In fact there is no reason why old women should not behave in this way – but if they did they would be considered 'eccentric'.
- The clothes she suggests are shocking because of their bright colours – our expectation is that old women should wear sober colours. She suggests spending her money on luxuries rather than on essentials – even though our expectation is that pensioners are not very 'well-off'. Her actions, e.g. sitting on the pavement, playing with a stick like a child, would be out of character with our expectations of 'the older generation'. Generally, the old woman wants to be an individual – not bound by the rules of society. She has to make up for the 'sobriety' of her youth. She will even carry out shocking things – stealing flowers, spitting, eating huge amounts of one thing.
- The scene is amusing because of the contrast of our expectations, but there is also a hint of sadness in the poem. She has been restricted all her life by what society says she must do. Even in her old age she has to follow rules – in fact, there may be even more rules for older people.

2 marks for point made fully.

d) Explain how the poet contrasts what people expect of an old woman with how she would like to behave.
4 marks

In your answer you should comment on:

- The final section of the poem gives an indication of what society expects, e.g. clothes should be to keep her dry, not colourful or shocking. Her money should be spent on practical things such as paying her rent, not on making her life pleasurable in its last stages. The way she speaks is even regulated by society's expectations, e.g. she is not expected to swear. Old people are expected to set a good example to the 'younger generation' and not act in outrageous ways. However, the younger generation are permitted to do this in some way. There is a sense that this was not always the case and this old woman seems to have 'missed out' on this. She will 'have friends to dinner'. **2 marks**
- All the earlier images – colourful clothes, shocking activities – are seen as in direct contrast to society's 'normal' rules. **1 mark**
- The woman is obviously not really old when she is writing the poem as she wants to 'practise' so people will not be too shocked later. There is a sense in which she has made up her mind to do some of these things. **1 mark**

Score	National Curriculum Level	
9 or 10	Level 7+	Exceptional answer
7 or 8	Level 7	Well above average answer
5 or 6	Level 6	Above average answer
3 or 4	Level 5	Average or below average answer
1 or 2	Level 4 or below	Well below average answer

Question 4

This question is marked for overall impression – there is not a set of correct points which should be incorporated. Both content and how the content is communicated – style, grammar, punctuation, accuracy – are considered.

However there is a set of marking criteria which need to be considered. Work through these with a parent or carer until you answer 'No'. This is the level at which you are working.

Does the answer:	Yes	No	Marks
Communicate ideas clearly to you?			6
Use a suitable style for the purpose indicated in the question?			6
Organise the material in an appropriate way to the style?			6
Use paragraphs, correct grammar and punctuation?			6
Spell words correctly and make use of relevant words precisely?			6
Look neat and make reading easy?			2

Score	National Curriculum Level
30–32	Level 7+
24–29	Level 7
18–23	Level 6
13–17	Level 5
7–12	Level 4 or below

Answers

All Shakespeare plays – Paper 2

This paper is marked for:

- **Understanding and Response**. What is written. This tests understanding of **the Shakespeare play**, its characters, its themes and story as well as its language.
- **Written Expression**. How it is written. This tests the candidate's ability to write clear answers about **the Shakespeare play** in clear, logical, grammatically correct English.

According to the official mark scheme there are 40 marks available for the Shakespeare section of the test.

- **Understanding and Response will be marked out of 24**

21–24 marks	Exceptional performance	Above Level 7
17–20 marks	Well above average	Level 7
13–16 marks	Above average	Level 6
9–12 marks	Average/below average	Level 5
4–8 marks	Well below average	Level 4 and below

- **Written Expression will be marked out of 16. See page 76 for details of this.**

Answers should include these key points, illustrated by suitable quotations.

Henry V

Key points – look for 6 of these and mark each out of 4

- The scene marks the public awareness of the authority of the king. Previously he had been thought of as Prince Hal – the young prince who spent a dissolute life in the taverns with his friends, including Falstaff, Pistol and Nym.
- Previously the French ambassador had arrived and had insulted him with the gift of tennis balls – to indicate that they thought he was still 'playful' and not to be treated seriously. However his response to them proved to the Lords present that he was serious about his country and was prepared to fight France.
- At the beginning of this scene we are aware that the king knows what the traitors have done: 'The king hath note of all that they intend'; so he is cleverly playing a part with them in order that they should incriminate themselves.
- Henry is more than polite to them at the start: 'my kind lord ... gentle night', which becomes ironic in the light of the fact that they are planning to kill Henry. He prompts them to make patriotic statements: 'Never was monarch better fear'd and loved', showing them to be hypocrites.
- He presents the traitors with a real case in law. The king is prepared to release the man who was arrested: 'we pardon him'. The traitors make a case for not showing mercy, 'lest example/Breed, by his sufferance'. They fall into Henry's trap and he cunningly and cleverly lets them. Note his continued pleasant yet bitter comments: 'in their dear care ...tender preservation of our person... I know your worthiness.' This is the king disappointed by traitors. He needs people he can trust about him.
- He hands them papers. The audience thinks they are official papers but they are a summary of their crimes: 'What see you in those papers that you lose/So much complexion?' He is in a sense torturing them and there should be a sense of enjoyment from now on.
- The lords beg for forgiveness – they ask for mercy in a way they have just denied for others. Henry's large speech is passionate and patriotic, showing his disgust of the traitors and his disappointment in them. He takes them one at a time and slowly lists their faults, 'Thou cruel/Ingrateful, savage and inhuman creature!' He calls them 'devils'.
- The traitors show their final respect for the King by humbly apologising. 'Beseeching God and you to pardon me'. He sentences them to death – it is necessary. He can show no mercy, judged by the traitors' own arguments.
- Like the true king that he is he switches directly to the matter in hand - the war in France. This gives some indication of how he will behave at the battle of Agincourt – caring for his men and their welfare but appealing to their patriotism in order to win the battle, 'Once more into the breach ...'

Twelfth Night

Key points – look for at least 6 of these and mark each out of 4

- In this extract from the scene we see the comic characters plotting to find ways of humiliating others and creating more confusion in the play. The characters are not aware of the confusing sub-plot which lies behind the story of Cesario/Viola. The plot of the challenge between Sir Andrew and the boy will bring the story to a head and ensure that the twins are brought face to face later in the play.
- Sir Toby is a comic character – fond of his drink – who lives at the house of Olivia. She tolerates him because he is a relative but we gain the impression that he is using his position for his own benefit. He is in love with Maria and it is she who thought up the plot against Malvolio.
- Malvolio is the puritan steward in the house of Olivia – very pompous and proud. He thinks he is above the rest – 'full of self love'. When he stops the loud singing and drinking session they are having one night – 'shall there be no more cakes and ale?' – Maria decides on revenge. She will use his worst self-deluding characteristics to trap him.
- Malvolio believes Olivia could love him, and when he finds the mysterious letter he follows the instructions meticulously – yellow stockings cross-gartered, always smiling, treating others with contempt, etc – 'go hang yourselves all! You are idle shallow things …'. This change of character is extremely funny but the others take it to extremes – 'we'll have him in a dark room and bound'. They 'shall make him mad indeed'
- Sir Andrew is a foolish knight and Sir Toby uses him mostly to waste his money. Sir Andrew is also deluded into thinking Olivia can love him. He has seen how Olivia is taken with the new messenger from the Duke – Cesario – and Sir Toby pressures him into writing a challenge to the youth. This is what he perceives as 'knightly' behaviour, but in reality he is a coward. Sir Toby is using him for sport, since he knows the young man, too, is a coward and it will be amusing to see them together; the letter 'comes from a clodpole'. Unfortunately for Sir Andrew, unknown to all, the true brother of Cesario/Viola is in the area and he is a fighter. When Sir Andrew later challenges the wrong man he receives a 'bloody coxcomb'. This is the painful end of the joke.
- Olivia is under the impression that she is in love with the young messenger from the Duke Orsino, whom she does not love. But the 'boy' is in fact a girl in disguise. This will create more confusion towards the end of the play when Viola's twin comes on the scene.
- Viola is aware of the Olivia's feelings but she can do nothing about the situation without revealing her true identity. She cannot do this because she herself is in love with the Duke.
- The play shows that love can be a delusion. The Duke thinks he loves Olivia, Olivia thinks she loves Cesario, Malvolio thinks Olivia loves him, Sir Andrew thinks Olivia loves him. Many of these people are victims of their own delusions, like Olivia and the Duke; others are victims of trickery and their inflated self-worth, like Sir Andrew and Malvolio. This causes comedy but also much unhappiness.
- Disguise leads to confusion in the play and many of the characters are not telling the truth or trying to be people they are not, like Cesario and Malvolio. This again is very amusing on stage but is painful to the characters – they suffer because of their delusions.

Macbeth

Key points – look for at least 6 of these and mark each out of 4

- In this scene, Banquo and Macbeth meet in the courtyard of Macbeth's castle. The king and his followers are staying at the castle and Banquo, as the loyal soldier, is standing guard with his son, Fleance.
- We are given some indication that Banquo is thinking about what the witches have previously told Macbeth and Banquo – 'A heavy summons lies like lead upon me'. He has 'cursed thoughts'. Macbeth is ironically 'a friend' although we know that later he is far from this. The two men have been comrades fighting together in the war for the king. Banquo 'dreamt last night of the three weird sisters' and Macbeth lies: 'I think not of them'. This indicates to us that the relationship between the two men has changed because of Macbeth's ambition and because he now sees Banquo as a threat.
- Earlier the three witches had told Macbeth he would be Thane of Cawdor and 'king hereafter'. These would seem to be impossible but when he finds out the king has given him the title of Cawdor, it crosses his mind that the final prophecy could come true. 'What, can the devil speak true? … the greatest is behind'. They have appealed to his innate ambition.
- Banquo is told he will 'get kings, though thou be none'. This again seems impossible, but if Macbeth is to take such a serious step as killing a king, he will need to know that his succession is assured. If Banquo's son Fleance is to be a king then what is the use of Macbeth's action? From this point Banquo becomes a threat and their relationship is altered for ever. Shakespeare shows us the power of evil and how it alters everything good in the world.
- Macbeth's final soliloquy in this scene shows us how he needs to call upon evil to hide the murder he is about to commit – 'witchcraft celebrates/Pale Hecate's offerings'. The dagger leads him to the king; he has not the strength to do this for himself. Lady Macbeth was right when she noted he was 'too full of the milk of human kindness'.
- After he has killed the Duncan and the Duncan's sons have fled from the scene, Macbeth becomes king but cannot rest because of his insecurity. 'It will have blood, they say blood will have blood.' He murders Banquo and attempts to murder Fleance, but Fleance escapes. Macduff flees to England and so Macbeth slaughters his wife and children.
- After Macbeth sees Banquo's ghost at the banquet, he returns to the witches to find out how evil can help him to secure his place on the throne. This time he enters into the evil ceremonies himself and the witches give him three more prophecies – glimpses of his future. The witches never directly lie to Macbeth but they allow him to delude himself. This time he feels that he is invincible. 'Beware the Thane of Fife' is met by killing his family. 'None of woman born/Shall harm Macbeth' appears to make him safe as all men are 'born of woman'. The third prophecy which states he will be safe until 'Great Birnham wood to high Dunsinane Hill/Shall come to him' also seems impossible. The witches delude him: Macduff had a caesarean birth, and the English soldiers cut branches and hold them in front of them for camouflage as they attack his castle (bringing 'Birnham wood' to Dunsinane).
- By the end of his life he is a changed person – 'I have almost forgot the taste of fear'. His wife is dead – she commits suicide and he does not seem to care: 'she should have died hereafter'. He is perceived as a tyrant, all his friends have left him. 'Life's but a walking shadow'. He realises that everything he has done has added up to nothing and he goes out purposefully to die at the hands of Macduff – 'I 'gin to be aweary of the sun'. From 'brave Macbeth', he has become a 'dead butcher'.

Checklist for Assessing Written Expression Levels 4–7

Work through this list with a parent or carer until you answer 'No'. This is the level at which you are working

Level 4	Yes	No	Marks
Ideas are clearly expressed			4
Paragraphs are used to organise ideas			
Punctuation to separate sentences is generally accurate			
Spelling of simple words is accurate			
Handwriting is clear and legible			

Level 5	Yes	No	Marks
Ideas are clearly expressed			8
Wide vocabulary, precise use of words			
Simple and complex sentences are used and made into paragraphs			
Variety of punctuation, apostrophes and commas are used correctly			
Complex and regular spelling patterns are used			
Handwriting is clear, legible and fluent			

Level 6	Yes	No	Marks
Ideas are clearly expressed with a sense of purpose			12
A varied vocabulary is used – appropriate language is expressed in simple and complex sentences with good paragraphing			
Spelling is accurate but some difficult words are still incorrect			
A range of punctuation is used – some more difficult forms			
Handwriting is fluent and legible			

Level 7	Yes	No	Marks
Confidently expressed ideas: the words chosen are appropriate			16
Appropriate style is matched by appropriate language			
Accurate grammar and punctuation are used consciously for effect			
Correct paragraphing and punctuation			
Spelling of irregular words is correct			
Handwriting is consistently fluent and legible			

Those achieving levels below level 4 or above level 7 should be obvious from their work if assessed on this chart. Those achieving above level 7 could be taking a supplementary test paper. Those achieving level 3 should be taking a special paper. It is best to consult a teacher.

National Curriculum Levels

The chart below gives an indication of performance in the combined English tests and provides a National Curriculum level.

Because the exam criteria for marking will change from year to year, depending on the difficulty of the test and the candidates involved, it is impossible to make this process exact.

Total the marks which have been given for both papers. The score will be out of 100.

- Paper 1 is marked out of 60.
- Paper 2 is marked out of 40.

Combined score of Papers 1 and 2	**Approximate National Curriculum Level**
29 and below	Below Level 4
30 – 45	Level 4
46 – 60	Level 5
61 – 75	Level 6
76 – 85	Level 7
86 and above	Above Level 7

If you need more practice in any English topics, use the WH Smith Key Stage 3 English Revision Guide.

Science at Key Stage 3

You can specifically improve your marks in Science by taking into account the following points:

The language used in the questions

1. The examiners will not put any useless information in a question. If something is written down then the examiner wants you to use it.
   - **Example:** *Space probes have shown that there are* ***mountains, dry river valleys*** *and* ***volcanoes*** *on Mars. Scientists believe Mars, ilke Earth, has all three types of rock:* ***igneous, metamorphic*** *and* ***sedimentary***. You will need to use all the terms.
2. Use the mark scheme to tell you how many points you should include in your answers.
3. Read the question very carefully.
   - **Example** *Tick the correct box.*
     Only tick one box. If you tick more than one box, the question will be marked incorrect.
4. Don't be put off if you encounter unfamiliar material. You will know enough science to answer the question. In the example above you may not know much about Mars. However, the work you have done on rock formation on Earth will let you answer the question.

Key words found in the questions

1. **Choose** from a list of words. Make sure you use words from the list. Unless the paper states otherwise, you can use words more than once. Similarly you don't have to use them all.
2. **Describe...** You do **not** have to explain anything; you simply have to make a physical description of a diagram, graph etc.
3. **Explain...** You need to include a scientific explanation for your answer. Include some key scientific words in your answer.
4. **Predict...** There are two possible types of prediction:
   - Predicting what you think might happen in an investigation.
   - Extrapolating a graph (continuing a trend) to predict what might happen in the future.
5. Be aware of **negatives**.
   Example: *Give the name of another metal,* ***not*** *in the table...*
6. **Advantages and disadvantages.** To be on the safe side, make sure you state both things in your comparisons.
7. **Name... Which... What... Give...** These are simple command words which require a simple response. These are often found with numbers or words in bold type.

Sitting the practice tests

These practice tests are designed to help you to get used to test conditions. When you take the tests in May you will be given an exact time (1 hour) and be expected to work in silence with no books or other person to help you. That is exactly how you should practise.

1. You need a pencil or pen and a watch or clock.
2. Ask someone to time the test so that you have exactly 60 minutes.
3. If you cannot read a scientific word then someone can read it to you. That person should not tell you what it means.
4. Do not start answering the questions until you have had a look at all of the test paper. This will give you a good idea of what is covered in the test and how many questions there are.
5. Read each question carefully and follow the instructions.
6. Do not spend too long over any one question. Answer it and move on.
7. If you can't answer a question, don't worry. Move on to the next one. You can always come back at the end.
8. Try to use all the time available. If you think you have finished, go back and check every question.
9. At the end of the time, check your answers with the mark scheme and work out your total.
10. Make a list of the questions you did not do too well on, but congratulate yourself on those you answered well.
11. Discuss the questions you found most difficult with a parent or a teacher. It is a good idea to check your notes to make sure that the topic won't cause problems again.
12. After a few weeks, try the questions again. You will improve your score if you have been working and revising and you will be well prepared for the real thing.

1 The information in the table shows the recommended daily amounts of nutrients and energy for different people.

Person	Energy	Protein	Iron	Calcium
Farm worker	12 000 Kj	60 g	10 mg	650 mg
Office worker	10 000 Kj	58 g	10 mg	650 mg
15 year-old boy	11 000 Kj	54 g	11 mg	950 mg
15 year-old girl	8 000 Kj	44 g	15 mg	800 mg
(approximate values)				

a Give one reason why the office worker needs a lower-energy diet than the farm worker.

____

____ 1

b Iron is needed to make red blood cells. Explain why 15 year-old girls need more iron than 15 year-old boys.

____

____ 1

c Give one reason why 15 year-old boys and girls need more calcium than adults.

____

____ 1

TOTAL 3

d i Which of the following foods would be the best source of calcium for the 15 year-olds?
Tick one box.

celery ☐ margarine ☐

milk ☐ chicken ☐

1

ii Which of the foods would be the best source of protein?
Tick one box.

celery ☐ margarine ☐

milk ☐ chicken ☐

1

iii Which of the foods would be the best source of fibre?
Tick one box.

celery ☐ margarine ☐

milk ☐ chicken ☐

1

TOTAL

3

2 The diagram shows an important organ system in females.

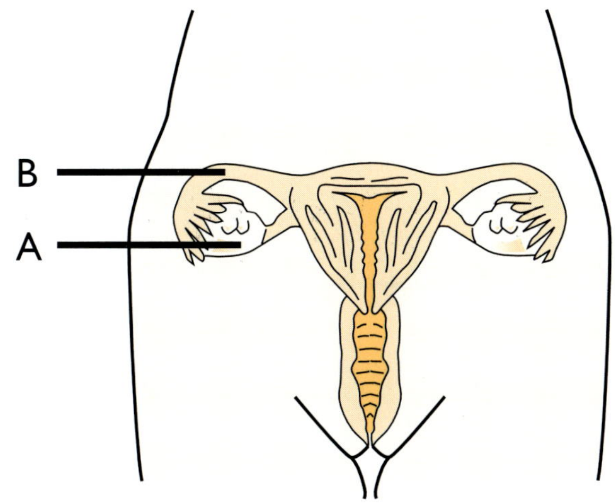

a What is the name of this organ system?

____ 1

b Eggs are produced in organ A. What is the name of organ A?

____ 1

c The eggs travel down tube B. What is the name of tube B?

____ 1

TOTAL

3

The diagram below shows the equivalent organ system in males.

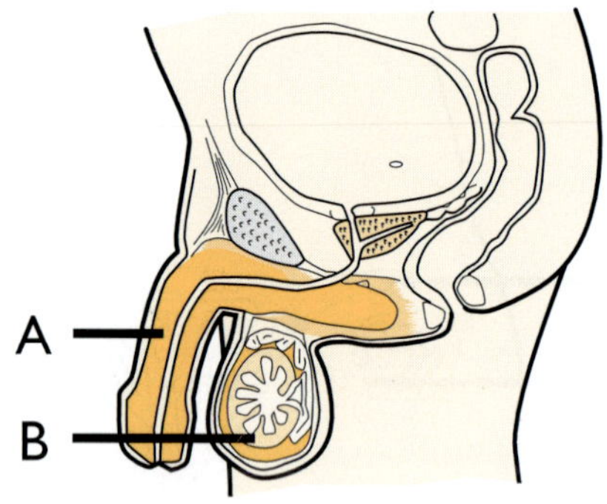

1

d What is organ A called?

____

1

e Sperm cells are made in organ B. What is organ B called?

____

6

f Use the words below to complete the description.

placenta	fertilised	embryo	divides	uterus	sperm

When ____________ cells meet an egg cell one of them will enter. The egg cell is ____________ . The egg cell then travels to the ____________ where it becomes embedded in the thick wall. The egg cell ____________ and develops into an ____________ . This is given food from the mother via the ____________ .

TOTAL

8

3a The diagram below shows human lungs.

i On the diagram write the names of A, B and C.

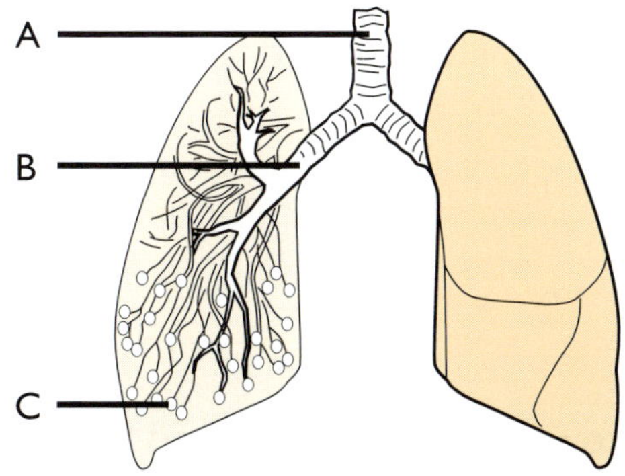

ii In each lung there are many branches. Each branch ends at the part you have labelled C.
Explain how this arrangement helps humans to breathe more effectively.

1

iii Part A has rings of material called cartilage. Suggest **one** reason why these rings of cartilage are present.

1

b The diagram shows an example of Part C in more detail.

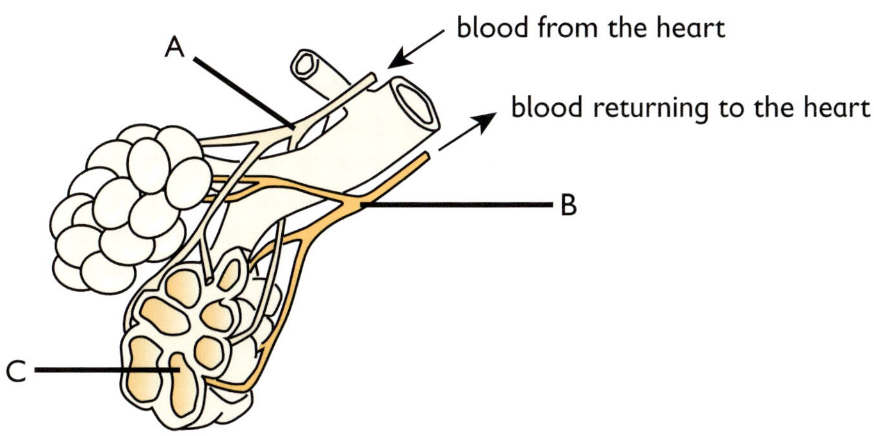

2

TOTAL

4

i Give one reason why part C has such a rich blood supply.

1

___

ii Describe **two** differences between the blood flowing in capillary A and the blood flowing in capillary B.

2

1. ___

2. ___

c Stewart was being tested for asthma. He was asked to breathe into a machine to test how much air he could breathe into and out of his lungs.

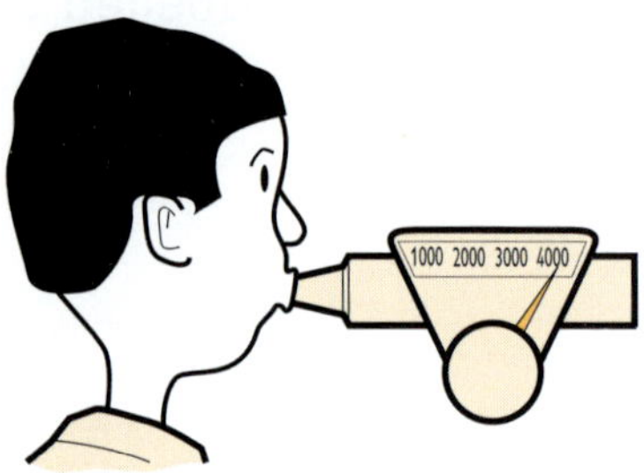

i How much air did Stewart manage to breathe out into the machine?

1

___

Air contains nitrogen, oxygen, carbon dioxide, noble gases and water vapour.

ii Give **two** differences between the composition of the air Stewart breathed in and the air he breathed out into the machine.

2

1. ___

2. ___

TOTAL

6

4 The diagram below shows the particles in a solid, liquid and gas.
Each arrow represents a change of state.

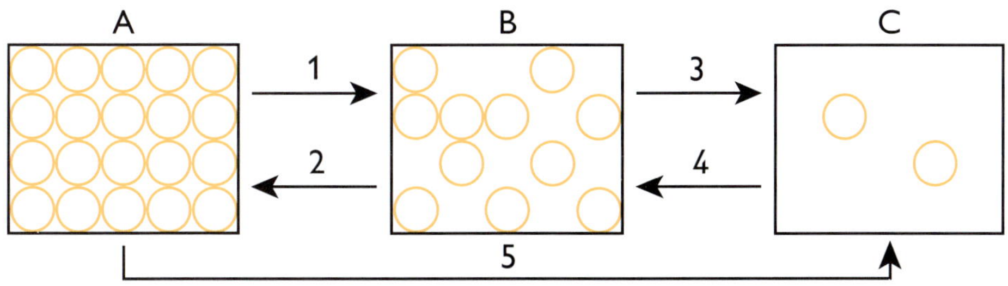

a Which diagram represents a solid?

____

Explain your answer.

____

____

1

1

b Which diagram represents a gas?

____

Explain your answer.

____

____

1

1

TOTAL

4

c Choose from the list of words to complete the sentences below.

condensation	sublimation	freezing
evaporation	boiling	melting

Change of state 1 is called ______________________

Change of state 2 is called ______________________

Change of state 3 is called ______________________

Change of state 4 is called ______________________

Change of state 5 is called ______________________

5

d Which change of state is being used during the following processes?

Separating water from salt by heating the water

____

Drying clothes on a washing line

____

Making ice cubes from water

____

3

TOTAL

8

5 The diagram below shows an investigation to examine rusting.

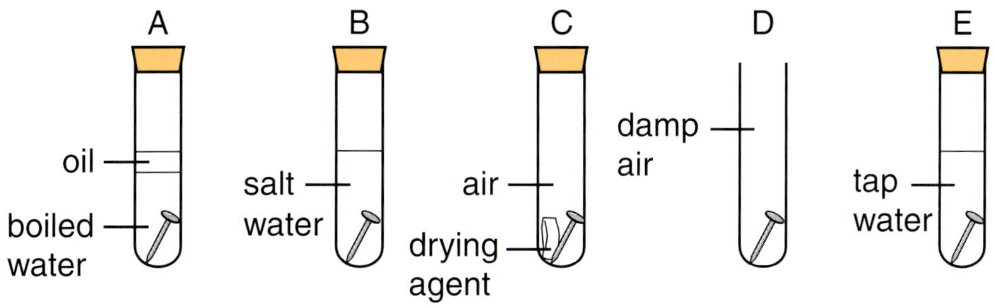

The table shows how each test tube was set up.

Tube	Treatment
A	A clean nail was covered with boiled water (to remove dissolved air) then covered with a layer of oil.
B	A clean nail was added to salty water.
C	A clean nail was added to a tube with air in. A drying agent was added to dry the air.
D	A clean nail was added to a tube of air, which was left open.
E	A clean nail was added to tap water.

All the tubes were then left for 5 days.

a Which nail would you expect to be the most rusty after 5 days?

The nail in tube ______________

Explain your answer.

____

____

2

TOTAL

2

b Which nail would you expect to be the least rusty after 5 days?

The nail in tube ____________________

Explain your answer.

____

____

2

c **i** Metal objects can be protected from rusting in a number of ways.
Write down **two** ways in which the nails in the rusting experiment could have been treated to stop them from rusting.

1. ____

2. ____

2

ii Rust is an oxide of iron. Which of the following words describes the formation of rust from iron?

condensation	reduction	oxidation	combustion

____

1

TOTAL

5

6 The table shows the names and chemical formulae of six naturally occurring substances.

name of substance	chemical formula
Malachite	$CuCO_3$
Marble	$CaCO_3$
Gold	Au
Bauxite	Al_2O_3
Diamond	C
Salt	NaCl

a From the table, give the name of **one** substance which is:

a carbonate ______________________________

a compound containing sodium ______________________________

a metallic element ______________________________

a non-metallic element ______________________________

an oxide of a metal ______________________________

5

TOTAL

5

6

b Below is a list of substances that occur naturally. Complete the table by putting ticks in the correct places.

Substance	element	compound	atom	molecule
O_2				
N_2				
CO_2				
Ne				
H_2O				
$CaCO_3$				

TOTAL

6

7a A tow truck is trying to pull a car along a level road.
The car's brakes are on and the car does not move.

i Draw **one** arrow on the diagram to show the direction of the force which prevents the car from moving. 1

ii Is the force of the pull of the tow truck **less than, equal to** or **more than** the force which prevents the car from moving? 1

____

b When the car's brakes are off, the tow truck pulls the wagon forwards. Another force (force X) works to slow the car down.

i What is the name of force X? 1

____

ii In what direction does this force act? 1

____

TOTAL 4

1

iii The pull of the tow truck is 4000 N. As the car's speed increases, how large is force X?

Tick the correct box.

More than 4000 N	☐	4000 N	☐
Between 0 and 4000 N	☐	zero	☐

1

iv After a few minutes, the car travels at a steady speed. The tow truck is still pulling with a force of 4000 N.

How large is force X now?

____

TOTAL

2

8 Fatima is trying to remove a wheel from her car. She is trying to release the wheel nuts with a spanner. The diagram shows the size of the force she is exerting and where the force acts on the spanner.

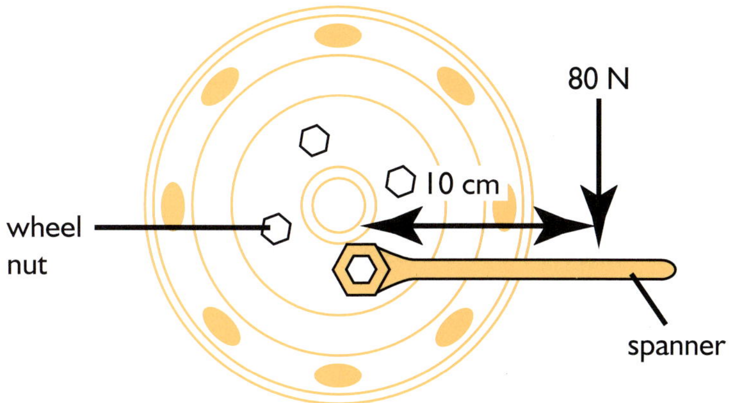

a The spanner applies a turning effect (moment) to the wheel nut. Calculate the size of the moment. Give the units.

2

b The wheel nut will not move. Give **two** ways in which Fatima could increase the moment she applies to the spanner.

1. ______________________________

2. ______________________________

2

TOTAL

4

9 Look at the circuit diagrams below:

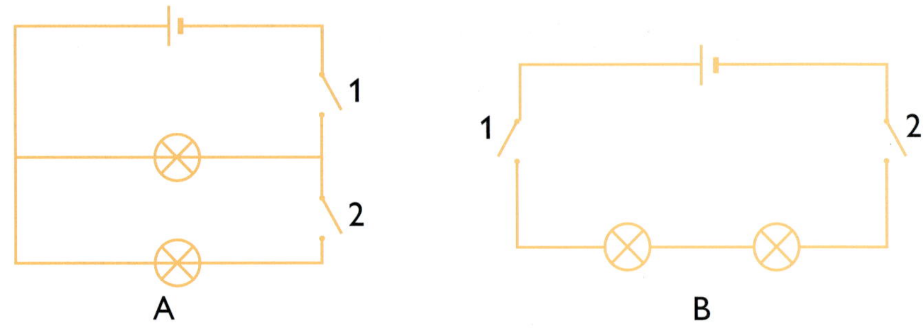

a Which circuit has the bulbs connected in series?

____

1

b If the currents flowing from the cells in A and B are the same:

i in which circuit will the bulbs be brightest?

____

1

ii If one of the bulbs in circuit B was blown, what would happen to the other?

____

1

iii Explain what you would see in circuit A if switch 1 was closed and switch 2 was open.

____

____

1

TOTAL

4

The same circuits were set up again but this time ammeters were added and the switches removed. Ammeters are devices for measuring current. The units used are called amperes or amps (A).

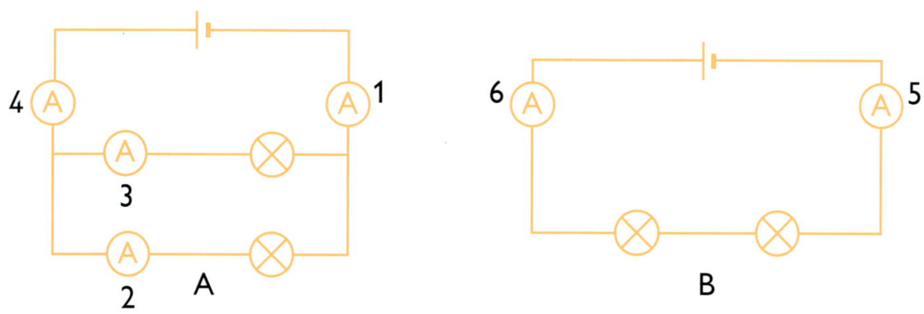

c **i** Complete the table by writing in the correct number of amps.

3

	Ammeter 1	Ammeter 2	Ammeter 3	Ammeter 4	Ammeter 5	Ammeter 6
Circuit A	2A	1A				
Circuit B					2A	

ii Explain your reason for all three answers.

____

____

____

2

TOTAL

5

10 The diagram shows part of a food web.

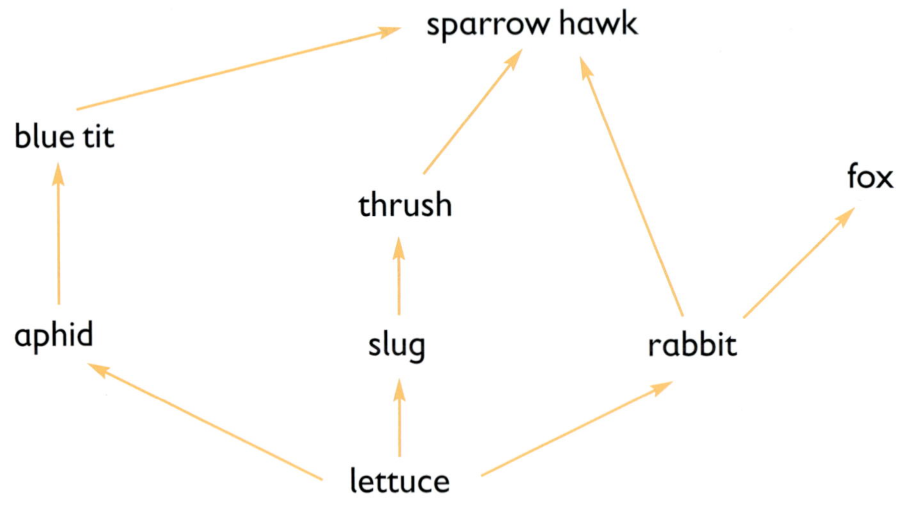

Use **only** the information in the diagram above to answer the following questions.

a Name **one** carnivore and **one** herbivore.

2

carnivore ______________________

herbivore ______________________

b A predator is an animal that catches smaller animals to eat. Give the name of one predator and the name of one of its prey.

2

predator ______________________

prey ______________________

TOTAL

4

c If the number of rabbits in a particular habitat decreases, this affects the numbers of other animals living there. Use the food web to explain:

i Why the number of slugs might increase.

____

____

1

ii Why the number of foxes might decrease.

____

____

1

iii Why the number of thrushes might increase.

____

____

1

iv Why the number of thrushes might decrease.

____

____

1

d The lettuce in the food web was sprayed with an insecticide. Explain why small amounts of the insecticide were found in the tissues of sparrow hawks.

____

____

1

TOTAL

5

11 The table below shows the pH of five common substances.

Substance	pH
Vinegar	3
Fruit juice	4
Pure water	7
Soap	8
Detergent	11

a Which two substances are acidic?

2

1. ______________________

2. ______________________

b Which two substances are alkaline?

2

1. ______________________

2. ______________________

c Which substance is neutral?

1

____

TOTAL

5

d Wasp stings are alkaline.
Which substance from the table could you rub on a wasp sting to stop it hurting?

2

____

Explain your answer.

____

____

e Sometimes soil is too acidic to allow certain crops to grow.
A farmer may decide to add lime to the soil to make the soil less acidic.

i Is lime an acid or an alkali?

1

____

____

ii Name the process of adding a substance to an acid to make the pH 7.

1

____

____

TOTAL

4

12

a can of cold cola in a fridge

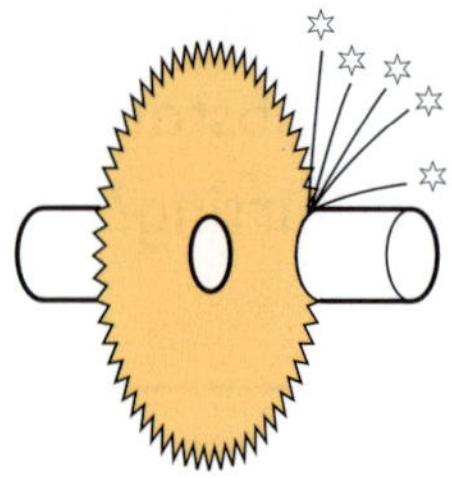

white-hot sparks from a cutter

a loop of wire glowing red-hot

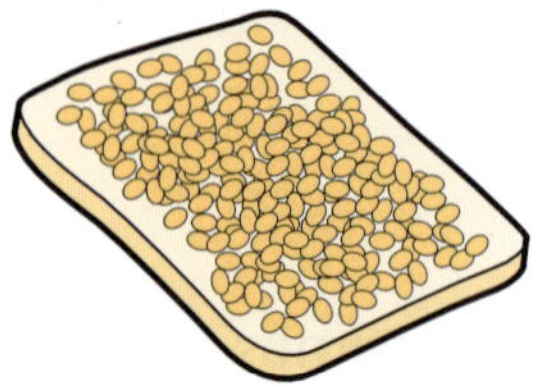

freshly cooked beans on toast

Each of the four objects shown above started at room temperature. Now they are all at different temperatures.

i Which object has lost thermal energy?

______________________________ 1

ii Which object has had the largest gain in thermal energy?

______________________________ 1

iii Which object is at the highest temperature?

______________________________ 1

TOTAL 3

b Samantha puts a hot spoon into a glass of water. She leaves it for ten minutes.

i What will happen to the temperature of the water during the ten minutes?

____ 1

Explain your answer.

____

____ 1

ii What will happen to the temperature of the spoon during the ten minutes?

____ 1

Explain your answer.

____

____

____ 1

TOTAL 4

c Look at the table below. Column 1 shows the thermal energy stored in the spoon and water before the experiment. Column 2 shows the thermal energy in the spoon and water after ten minutes.

	1	2
	before	**after ten minutes**
Spoon	9800 J	6800 J
Water	4400 J	6800 J

i Calculate how many joules of energy the spoon loses during the ten minutes.

1

ii Calculate how many joules of energy have been gained by the water during the ten minutes.

1

iii Calculate the difference between the loss of energy from the spoon and the gain in energy by the water.

1

iv What has happened to the energy in part iii?

1

TOTAL

4

Question number	Answer	Mark
1a	An office worker will not be moving around as much and so will need less energy.	1
1b	Some 15 year-old girls have started menstruation and so will lose blood every month.	1
1c	15 year-old boys and girls are still growing and need calcium for bones.	1
1d	i milk ii chicken iii celery	1 1 1
2a	reproductive system	1
2b	ovary	1
2c	oviduct *or* fallopian tube	1
2d	penis	1
2e	testicle	1
2f	sperm, fertilised, uterus, divides, embryo, placenta	6
3a	i trachea bronchus alveolus ii The alveoli increase the surface area of the lungs. iii To strengthen the trachea and stop it from collapsing.	2 1 1
3b	i To let gases into and out of the blood. ii 1. Blood in capillary A has more carbon dioxide. 2. Blood in capillary A has less oxygen.	1 2
3c	i 4000 cm^3 ii 1. The air he breathed in was richer in oxygen than the air he breathed out. 2. The air he breathed out was richer in carbon dioxide than the air he breathed in.	1 2
4a	A The particles are closely packed together.	1 1
4b	C The particles are very far apart.	1 1
4c	1 = melting, 2 = freezing, 3 = evaporation or boiling, 4 = condensation, 5 = sublimation	5

Question number	Answer	Mark
4d	evaporation or boiling evaporation freezing	3
5a	B Salt makes things rust faster.	2
5b	A Rusting needs oxygen and water, and tube A has little oxygen in it.	2
5c	i Any two from painting/oiling/coating with a more reactive metal such as zinc. ii oxidation	2 1
6a	malachite *or* marble salt gold diamond (carbon) bauxite	5
6b	element and molecule element and molecule compound element and atom compound compound	6
7a	i Therre should be an arrow above the car pointing left (opposite to the arrow already on the diagram). ii equal	1 1
7b	i gravity ii downwards iii between 0 and 4000 N iv 4000 N	1 1 1 1
8a	80 N x 10 cm = 800 Ncm	2
8b	1. Increase the force she applies. 2. Apply the force further away from the fulcrum (pivot).	2
9a	B	1
9b	i. A ii. The other bulb would go out. iii. Only one bulb would light – the one nearest to the battery.	1 1 1
9c	i. Circuit A Ammeter 3 = 1A Ammeter 4 = 2A Circuit B Ammeter 6 = 2A	3

Question number	Answer	Mark
	ii The parallel circuit allows the two bulbs to share the current and so each branch will have 1A. The current in the series circuit is the same throughout.	2
10a	sparrow hawk, fox, blue tit or thrush slug, aphid or rabbit	2
10b	predator = sparrow hawk prey = blue tit/thrush/rabbit or predator = fox prey = rabbit or predator = thrush prey = slug	2
10c	i. There will less competition for lettuce. ii. There will not be enough food to support the population. iii. More slugs could result in an increased population of thrushes. iv. Sparrow hawks might catch more thrushes as there are fewer rabbits.	1 1 1 1
10d	The insecticide was passed from lettuce to slugs then from slugs to thrushes and finally to sparrow hawks as the various living things were eaten.	1
11a	1. vinegar 2. fruit juice	2
11b	1. soap 2. detergent	2
11c	pure water	1
11d	vinegar or fruit juice The acidic substance will neutralise the alkaline sting.	2
11e	i. alkali ii. neutralisation	1 1
12a	i. can of cola ii. white-hot sparks from a cutter iii. white-hot sparks from a cutter	1 1 1
12b	i. It will rise. Thermal energy from the spoon will heat the water. ii. It will fall. Thermal energy is lost to the cooler water.	1 1 1 1
12c	i. 3000 J ii. 2400 J iii. 600 J iv. It has been given out to the environment as heat.	1 1 1 1

National Curriculum Levels

Maximum marks: 105

Mark	0–40	41–56	57–72	73–91	92–105
Level	Below Level 4	Level 4	Level 5	Level 6	Level 7

If you need more practice in any Science topics, you should use the WHSmith Key Stage 3 Science Revision Guide.